The Guide to
Colorado Reptiles
and Amphibians

Mary Taylor Young

Photographs by Lauren J. Livo and Steve Wilcox

FULCRUM
GOLDEN, COLORADO

Library of Congress Cataloging-in-Publication Data
Young, Mary Taylor, 1955-
   The guide to Colorado reptiles and amphibians / By Mary Taylor Young ;
photographs by Lauren J. Livo and Steve Wilcox.
       p. cm.
   Includes bibliographical references and index.
   ISBN 978-1-55591-584-1 (pbk. : alk. paper) 1. Reptiles--Colorado. 2.
Amphibians--Colorado. I. Title.
   QL653.C6Y68 2011
   597.909788--dc22

                              2010040141

Printed in Korea
0 9 8 7 6 5 4 3 2 1

Design: Jack Lenzo
Cover image: Lauren J. Livo, *Crotaphytus collaris* eastern collared lizards

Fulcrum Publishing
4690 Table Mountain Drive, Suite 100
Golden, Colorado 80403
800-992-2908 • 303-277-1623
www.fulcrumbooks.com

Contents

REPTILES – CLASS REPTILIA

Acknowledgments

The metamorphosis of this book from tadpole to frog came about with the help of others. Thanks go to top-notch herpetologist Lauren Livo for her early input on the species list and for reviewing the text, as well as for the wonderful photography she and her husband, Steve Wilcox, provided. Kudos to Tina Jackson, state herpetologist with the Colorado Division of Wildlife, for her support and enthusiasm and for reviewing the manuscript (and for having a charming pet box turtle named Turtle). Thanks to Derek Lawrence, Faith Marcovecchio, and the other folks at Fulcrum Publishing for supporting this book and in that way, supporting the wildlife of our state. I thank Geoffrey A. Hammerson for his excellent book *Amphibians and Reptiles in Colorado*, which was a wonderful resource—a thorough and technical guide for anyone interested in delving deeper into the biology and life history of Colorado reptiles and amphibians.

Introduction

We've all encountered reptiles and amphibians, maybe a turtle lumbering across a country road, a frog hopping with a splash into a pond, a snake slithering through the grass at our feet. As kids, many of us brought home a toad in our pocket as a gift for Mom. There's something about these creeping, crawling, darting creatures that fascinates us and brings an element of surprise, delight, and whimsy to outings in the Colorado outdoors.

Habitats in Colorado range from under 4,000 feet at the Kansas border to above 14,000 feet atop the highest peaks. A variety of reptiles and amphibians inhabit this 10,000-foot elevation spread. The ponds and creeks of the Eastern Plains are home to a variety of snakes, turtles, frogs, and toads. Western canyons provide habitat for various lizards and snakes, and species that tolerate dry conditions. While few reptiles are found above 6,000 feet, some hardy amphibians, including wood frogs, boreal toads, and boreal chorus frogs, survive in the most austere conditions amid alpine wetlands and ponds at the highest elevations in the state. Colorado's lone salamander, the barred tiger salamander, is found statewide, from the lowest to highest elevations. More than 70 species of reptiles and amphibians live in the many habitats in between.

The Guide to Colorado Reptiles and Amphibians will help readers discover many of these fascinating herptiles. This nature guide is written for a general audience so that kids, families, and creepy-crawlie fans of all persuasions can read it and use it in the field. I hope that by discovering and learning more about these quirky and fascinating creatures, readers will also become advocates for their protection and conservation.

Reptiles + Amphibians = Herptiles

Reptiles and amphibians are often lumped together. Both groups are cold blooded and lack either feathers or fur, so they don't seem very warm and cuddly. Since many of them crawl or scurry, we often characterize them as "creepy-crawlies." Even biologists lump them together under the terms *herptiles* or *herpetofauna* (with the nickname *herps*). The scientists who study them are called herpetologists. The root of the word comes from the Greek word *herpeton*, meaning "a creature that creeps or crawls." But reptiles and amphibians each belong to a different animal class. Reptiles, class Reptilia, have dry, scaly skin and breathe air throughout their life. Amphibians, grouped into the class Amphibia, typically have moist, slimy skin, require water for breeding, and undergo a metamorphosis from water-breathing, fishlike larva to air-breathing, four-legged adult.

How Animals Are Related

Biologists classify animals in a cascading taxonomic system of categories, from general to specific, that every beginning biology student must memorize: kingdom, phylum, class, order, family, genus, species. (These classifications are further broken down into subfamily, subspecies, and so forth.) Thus, an ornate box turtle would be categorized in the following way:

Kingdom: Animalia (animals rather than plants)
Phylum: Chordata (animals with a backbone)
Class: Reptilia (reptiles, as opposed to fish, amphibians, birds, or mammals)
Order: Testudines (turtles)
Family: Emydidae (pond and box turtles)
Genus: *Terrapene* (box turtles)
Species: *ornata* (ornate box turtle)

Colorado is home to about 71 species of reptiles and amphibians, though this can change with new information and discoveries.

How to Look for Reptiles and Amphibians

We often find reptiles and amphibians by accident, coming across them in the course of hiking or exploring. We can increase our chances of finding them by knowing the habitats in which they live and understanding their activity patterns and seasonal behaviors.

Spring through fall is reptile and amphibian season. Because they are cold blooded, meaning they derive warmth from their surroundings, these animals are largely inactive during the cold months of the year and during cool times of day. They hibernate during winter, though some become active on warm, sunny winter days.

Reptiles are sun-loving creatures, and many bask to elevate their body temperature, especially in the morning, when they emerge from cool, sheltered spots. If you visit a wetland or pond, approach slowly and look for turtles basking on logs, hummocks, and banks. Rocks and outcrops are good places to spot basking lizards. Snakes often slither onto roads, trails, and patches of open, dark-colored soil to warm up.

The spring breeding season offers some fun chances to see—and hear—interesting behaviors. In evening, early morning, and sometimes during the day, frogs and toads sing in breeding ponds and wetlands to attract mates. The sound can be deafening. But step to the edge of the pond, and the croaking will stop like someone flipped a switch. Sit quietly, and the animals will come to the surface and begin calling again. Watch as they inflate the vocal sacs on their throats like enormous balloons.

Lizards are fairly tolerant of being approached. You may be rewarded with the sight of competing males doing push-ups or body lifts to flash their breeding colors and challenge each other. They may rush at and chase each other.

Driving country roads in the evening, especially after a rain, is a good way to find reptiles and amphibians. As the air cools, snakes often move onto warm roadways. Frogs, toads, and turtles may also move across roadways as they migrate to breeding areas. Be very careful not to run over them. Thousands of snakes, turtles, frogs, and toads are killed by vehicles every year. Centuries of adaptation have not prepared these animals for the obstacles of roads built through their habitat. A turtle's shell is poor defense against a speeding car.

Reptiles and amphibians are often secretive creatures that hide under rocks and logs. If you turn over sheltering objects in your search, be sure to replace the objects where they originally lay to protect both vertebrates and invertebrates hidden there. Be very careful. You may startle a rattlesnake. If you hear a rattle, back out of striking distance. Given an escape option, rattlesnakes will usually flee. Many nonvenomous snakes, such as bullsnakes, mimic rattlesnakes by hissing or vibrating their tails against dry vegetation.

If you pick up an animal, handle it gently. These creatures are small and delicate, and can easily be injured by rough handling. For your protection and the animal's, wear gloves. Remember to wet your hands before handling an amphibian to preserve the protective mucous on its skin. After examining a reptile or amphibian, release it where you collected it. Crouch down and allow the animal to escape from your hands onto the ground. Don't drop it from a height, and don't grab snakes by the tail and fling them. Naturally, it is unwise to handle venomous snakes.

Don't Take Them Home

That horned lizard that looks like a tiny triceratops is so cute it would make an ideal pet, right? Wrong. Reptiles and amphibians are often difficult to maintain in captivity. They have specialized nutritional needs, and even the best-intentioned people often don't understand how to care for them.

Collecting or possessing most native Colorado reptiles and amphibians is against the law without a special license. These small creatures are an important component of the Colorado landscape and should be left in the wild.

Larval tiger salamanders, bullfrogs, snapping turtles, and prairie rattlesnakes may be taken as game or for use as bait with a valid small-game or fishing license. Seventeen nongame species that are relatively abundant can be possessed for noncommercial purposes. It is illegal to sell, trade, or barter these animals. Check the Legal Status in each Species Account for the rules of possession.

If you can't resist bringing one of the allowed herptiles home, don't do it on a whim. These animals are not toys. Collecting them carries responsibility. Visit pet stores and do research to learn how to care for them. Construct an appropriate habitat—and that usually means more than a wooden crate or small aquarium. Be prepared for a long-term commitment. Many herptiles live for decades, far longer than human interest in them lasts. Some turtles live 150 years!

If you want to release a collected animal into the wild, do it as close as possible to the spot where you picked it up, near cover it can dart under. Do this well before cold weather sets in to allow the animal time to find a secure hibernaculum and get ready for hibernation. If you release the animal in an unfamiliar location, there is a much higher chance it will die from starvation, exposure, or predation. To avoid spreading disease, don't release animals that have been in contact with herptiles from other areas. And don't release nonnative animals into the wild. Find a home for them with a responsible herptile collector or contact a herptile rescue organization such as the Colorado Reptile Humane Society at www.corhs.org.

Reptiles and Amphibians in Trouble

Though the boys throw stones at frogs in sport, yet the frogs do not die in sport, but in earnest.
— Bion of Borysthenes, Greek writer, ca. 300 BC

It isn't easy being green, according to Kermit the Frog, and things aren't looking good for herptiles of any color.

Land and resource development in Colorado have spelled trouble for many reptiles and amphibians. Wetlands being drained; rivers and streams being dammed; pollutants from agriculture, mining, and urban development running off into waterways; habitat being converted to farms, towns, and cities; the introduction of nonnative predatory species into waterways—all of these changes have made life hard for many native herptiles. Native reptiles and amphibians have largely disappeared from many urban and suburban landscapes.

Biologists are especially concerned about amphibian populations, both in Colorado and globally. Since the 1980s, 120 amphibian species have gone extinct worldwide, and a third of all amphibians are considered in danger. Sudden die-offs and the disappearance of entire populations of frogs and toads, as well as an increase in abnormalities such as frogs developing extra legs, have experts scrambling to find the causes.

A major culprit is the amphibian chytrid (KIT-trid) fungus, which grows on the permeable skin of amphibians and makes the skin unable to absorb water. This fungus has been blamed for wiping out frog populations all over the world. Pesticides and other toxins and pollutants in water also lead to amphibian die-offs and a much higher occurrence of deformed amphibians. Because the metamorphosis of amphibians takes place externally, rather than inside an egg or womb, development is more easily affected by elements in the environment. Research on causes of amphibian declines and malformations, and possible remedies for them, is ongoing.

There are currently 16 Colorado herptiles classified as species of special concern, as noted in the Legal Status section of each Species Account. This classification may be due to declining populations or because not enough is known about an uncommon species to determine if its population is stable or declining.

Presently, the only endangered herptile in Colorado is the boreal toad, also known as the mountain or western toad.

How to Use This Book

The intention of this book is to help readers discover and learn more about Colorado's native reptiles and amphibians. There are other reptile and amphibian guidebooks on the market, but they are either too technical for a general audience or include all the species found in North America. For example, there are 112 species of salamanders north of Mexico, but only one of those lives in Colorado. Why plow through all that extra information?

This guide is written for casual naturalists, outdoor recreationists, families, Colorado vacationers, and anyone desiring a general overview and identification guide for creatures seen in the wild. Positive identification of species often requires study and measurement of anatomical features of specimens collected in the field. For more information on how to tell similar species apart, see the chart on pages 163–64. For further and more detailed biological information, readers should consult a reference such as *Amphibians and Reptiles in Colorado* by Geoffrey A. Hammerson, a technical but highly informative text.

Species Accounts

Within this book, each reptile or amphibian species inhabiting Colorado is described within a Species Account. Species

are arranged by taxonomic order (explained in the How Animals Are Related section on page 2). Amphibians are discussed first, leading with the state's lone salamander and working through the toads and frogs. They are followed by reptiles—first turtles, then lizards, then snakes. Color tabs on each page are used to denote animal family: yellow for salamanders, light green for spadefoot toads, and so on. Each animal is then described with the following information:

Common Name and *Scientific Name* are derived from the Society for the Study of Amphibians and Reptiles (SSAR) list of *Scientific and Standard English Names of Amphibians and Reptiles of North America North of Mexico*, Sixth Ed., 2008. (http://ssar herps.org/pages/HerpCommNames.php). Common names not used by SSAR but widely recognized (such as the bullsnake) are featured first. Where the animal is identified as a particular subspecies, that name is reflected in the scientific name.

Field ID is a physical description of the adult form of the animal, unless otherwise noted.

Size is the range, in inches and centimeters, of adult animals, from the average size at sexual maturity to the maximum size. Measurements for the tiger salamander, the lizards, and snakes are given as total length (TL) from tip of nose to tip of tail. Measurements for frogs and toads are for snout–vent length (SVL) from the tip of the snout to the vent (anal opening). Measurements for turtles are for carapace length (CL), the length of the upper shell from front edge to back edge.

Habitat describes the landscapes and plant communities the animal inhabits in Colorado.

Distribution is the geographic range in which the species is found within the state, including elevation range.

Field Notes discusses life history, physical characteristics, behavior, and other interesting information. Technical terms mentioned in the text are defined in the glossary at the back of the book.

Legal Status is the classification by the Colorado Division of Wildlife (CDOW). Nongame animals are protected by state law and cannot be killed, collected, or possessed without a special collector's license, except as indicated. The four game species can be taken with a state small-game or fishing license, as indicated. Species of special concern have no additional protections beyond the nongame designation but are being monitored because their populations may be declining. The only endangered species, the boreal toad (also called the mountain or western toad), is protected by law because its populations have declined significantly and it may be in imminent danger of disappearing from our state. Boreal toads cannot be killed, harmed, collected, disturbed, or harassed. This information and each species' legal status can change at any time, so please check with CDOW before collecting any animals.

Each species acount includes a range map, showing the Colorado counties in which the species has been found. Blue indicates known occurence. Green indicates likely occurence.

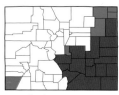

Coachwhip
Coluber flagellum

Scattered throughout the Species Accounts are sidebars highlighting interesting information about amphibian and reptile biology, life history, and behavior.

A glossary of terms used to discuss amphibians and reptiles follows the Species Accounts.

A checklist of Colorado amphibians and reptiles lists all species found in the state, by family.

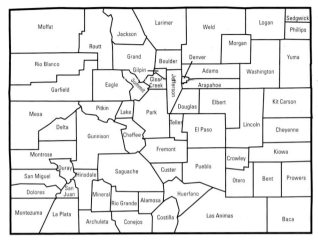

Colorado counties

AMPHIBIANS
CLASS AMPHIBIA

What Is an Amphibian?

Amphibians have long fascinated humans because of the miraculous metamorphosis they undergo. Beginning life as creatures with gills that live in water, they evolve into creatures that breathe air and live on land. Amphibians were the first land-dwelling vertebrates. As the link between fish and reptiles, they are living examples of the evolution of life-forms from water-dwelling to land-dwelling.

Biologists categorize amphibians within the class Amphibia. This class includes salamanders, frogs, and toads (and the tropical caecilians). Amphibians are not as abundant in our arid state as reptiles, because they are reliant on water for breeding. There is one species of salamander native to Colorado, along with seven species of frogs and ten species of toads.

Characteristics of Amphibians

Typically, there are three stages to amphibian life history: egg, larva, and adult. Amphibian eggs are surrounded by a jellylike material and must be laid in water. With most frogs and toads, eggs are fertilized externally. Most salamanders have internal fertilization in which the female takes up sperm deposited by the male.

Eggs hatch into fishlike larvae, whimsically called tadpoles or polliwogs. At metamorphosis, the larvae undergo a startling physical transformation, replacing gills with lungs, shedding tail for legs, and crawling from the water to complete the adult stage of life on land. The length of the larval stage varies by species and environmental conditions. In arid habitats with brief wet periods and ephemeral ponds, larvae must grow and undergo metamorphosis quickly. Many adult amphibians live close to water and spend a lot of time immersed because of the need to keep their skin moist.

Amphibians (except for the caecilians, found in the tropics) have naked, moist skin that is not protected by scales, feathers, or fur. To avoid drying out, amphibians must sit in water or on moist soil and absorb moisture through their permeable skin. They can also "breathe" through their skin, absorbing oxygen into blood vessels just beneath it. While most amphibians must live in or near water, some, like the spadefoot toads of the Eastern Plains, have adapted to arid habitats by burrowing into moist soil or under rocks and becoming inactive through much of the year.

Glands in the skin secrete mucous that keeps the skin moist and protects the animal from drying out. The slimy mucous also makes the animal difficult for a predator to grasp. Even with this mucous layer, most amphibians dehydrate quickly away from a moist environment. When handling amphibians, always wet your hands first to protect the mucous layer.

Amphibians are ectothermic, or cold blooded, meaning they derive body heat from the environment rather than generating it internally, as mammals and birds do. Because of this, they become sluggish in cool weather and must hibernate in winter.

SALAMANDERS: ORDER CAUDATA

Salamanders are abundant in other parts of the United States, but Colorado is home to only a single species.

These creatures are lizardlike in appearance, with long, low bodies and long tails. They are nocturnal, secretive, and silent, much less conspicuous and familiar than their amphibian relatives the frogs and toads. This order includes newts, mudpuppies, mole salamanders, lungless salamanders, and the two-and-a-half-foot giant salamander known as the hellbender.

Note: Measurements for the tiger salamander are for its total length (TL), from tip of nose to tip of tail.

Family Ambystomatidae – Mole Salamanders

This group of salamanders lives in North America, but only a single species, the barred tiger salamander, inhabits Colorado. Mole salamanders have stocky bodies, sturdy legs, and short, broad heads with blunt muzzles. The larvae have wide heads with feathery gills trailing from either side. Tiger salamanders are the largest of the mole salamander group.

As you might gather from their name, mole salamanders are good burrowers. The adults live on land, and both adults and larvae are carnivorous. Courtship and breeding happen spring through late summer, and unlike in frogs and toads, fertilization is internal. Some larvae are capable of breeding even without completing metamorphosis to the adult stage.

Barred Tiger Salamander
Ambystoma mavortium

Field ID: Large head; long body with smooth, slightly slimy skin; long tail; blunt nose. Feet lack claws. Color pattern varies from black with yellow bars and blotches to dark cream or olive with black blotches. Individuals that have not completed metamorphosis have feathery gills projecting from each side of their neck. **Size:** 6–13½ inches (15.2–34.3 cm).

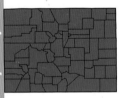

Habitat: Small ponds, seasonal pools, drainage ditches, runoff puddles, moist spots beneath logs and rocks, animal burrows and other hidden places.

Distribution: Throughout the state, up to about 12,000 feet.

Field Notes: The tiger is Colorado's lone salamander, named for its characteristic yellow-and-black color pattern. It is able to survive wherever sufficient moisture accumulates, even in seasonal pools on the Eastern Plains. Salamanders are active mainly at night from March through November. They are preyed on by fish, bullfrogs, birds, turtles, and crayfish. In turn they hunt earthworms, insects, and, occasionally, small rodents. They may gather in large numbers in the many fish-less stock and retaining ponds created throughout the state. They are usually missing from ponds with bullfrogs, crayfish, carnivorous fish, and other predators that feed on the adults and larvae.

Legal Status: Game species. Daily bag limit of up to 50 gilled larvae less than 5 inches long and four adults. May be harvested or possessed for use as bait with a valid fishing license.

Knee-ott-uh-knee?

Okay, so the word is really *neoteny*, and it describes the ability of some salamanders, including the barred tiger salamander, to become sexually mature and produce offspring without undergoing metamorphosis. These neotenes remain as water-dwelling larvae, with gills and fins, though they also develop lungs. High altitude, dry climate, and a lack of iodine in the water can lead to neoteny. If conditions change, the larval salamander may complete metamorphosis to the adult form. High-mountain and alpine lakes are good places to check for neotenes.

What Is a Salamander?

At first glance, a salamander looks a lot like a lizard. It has a long body, a long tail, and a longer snout than a frog or toad has. Despite this superficial resemblance, a salamander is an amphibian, while a lizard is a reptile. Salamanders have smooth, moist skin, no claws on their toes, and undergo metamorphosis. The barred tiger salamander is the only salamander native to Colorado.

FROGS AND TOADS: ORDER ANURA

This largest order of amphibians includes frogs and toads, familiar animals that even the youngest child can recognize. They have loose skin, no tail, usually no ribs, but a bony girdle around the chest. The legs are well developed, the hind legs much longer than the front. They have good ears, and males of most species produce a variety of songs and vocalizations. As adults, Colorado's anurans live on land or in the water but must return to water to breed. Unlike salamanders, none of the anurans stays in the larval form. Adults are carnivorous.

Note: Measurements for frogs and toads are for snout–vent length (SVL), from the tip of the snout to the vent (anal opening).

Family: Scaphiopodidae – Spadefoot Toads

Spadefoot toads are named for the dark, horny, sharp-edged projection, or tubercle, on the inside of each hind foot. They use this "spade" for digging (backward) into the soil, where they shelter themselves from extreme heat and dryness. Some of these toads have a lump, or boss, between the eyes and a parotoid gland (not externally visible), which secretes a toxin to deter predators, behind each eye. They have teeth in the upper jaw but not the lower, and thinner skin than other toads. Adults have "cat eyes," with vertical, oval pupils when seen in dim light.

This family is adapted to dry habitats. They live on land and only enter water during their brief breeding season, when spring rains draw them from underground burrows. At that time, the loud, bawling call of the males can be heard from a long distance. Because the seasonal pools they breed in will soon dry up, spadefoot toads mature very rapidly, some species going from egg to metamorphosis within one to two weeks. As their habitat dries, they reenter their burrows and may spend up to 10 months of the year underground. During hibernation, they can lose up to half their body weight.

Couch's Spadefoot
Scaphiopus couchii

Field ID: Moderate-sized, plump toad. Greenish yellow with dark spots or mottling, white belly, and an elongated spade on each hind foot. No boss between eyes. Eyes have vertical pupils; adult females' have a network of dark patterning. **Size:** 2¼–3½ inches (5.7–8.9 cm).

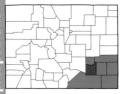

Habitat: Shortgrass prairie.

Distribution: Southeastern Colorado along the Arkansas River and its tributaries.

Field Notes: Couch's spadefoot toads are rare in Colorado. They weren't found in the state until 1977. They survive in the arid habitat of the Colorado prairie by spending much of their life burrowed into the soil, where they can survive for long periods, even when it is extremely dry. They emerge with the rains of spring and become active from late April or May through early October, depending on moisture conditions. The breeding calls of the males sound like a bleating lamb, with each call lasting about one second. Choruses of Couch's spadefoots can be heard from a long way off. These toads have adapted to take advantage of seasonal ponds, which can dry up quickly. Their eggs may hatch within 36 hours of being laid, and the tadpoles can metamorphose just eight days after hatching.

Legal Status: Species of special concern.

Plains Spadefoot
Spea bombifrons

Field ID: Small, stout-bodied toad. Gray to brown with a greenish tinge and orange warts. Hard lump on top of head directly between the eyes, which have vertical pupils. Each hind foot has a wedge-shaped spade. Hourglass pattern on back. **Size:** 1½–2½ inches (3.8–6.4 cm).

Habitat: Shortgrass prairie, sandhills, shrublands.

Distribution: Throughout the Eastern Plains, up to about 6,000 feet, and in the San Luis Valley.

Field Notes: This small toad is well adapted to life on the dry grasslands of Colorado. It is active mainly at night, when humidity is higher. To seek shelter from the elements or when it hibernates, it uses the sharp bump, or spade, on its hind foot to burrow backward into the prairie soil. Spring rains bring these toads from their burrows for breeding. The male's mating call is a hoarse, grating sound lasting about a second. Because the pools they breed in may soon dry up, their eggs and tadpoles develop quickly. Eggs may hatch within 48 hours. The total time of development, from laying of eggs through metamorphosis to adult, may take as little as two weeks. The toads are active from late April through the end of August, with some still active through September.

Legal Status: Nongame species. Up to four individuals can be taken and possessed without a license for noncommercial purposes, though no more than 12 individuals in total of all animals from the list of allowed species can be possessed at any one time.

Buried Alive

Spadefoot toads spend much of their lives buried in the soil. They use the spades on their hind feet to burrow backward into the ground, where they may live for eight to ten months of the year. By hibernating in these relatively moist dens, they are able to survive in very dry habitats. Spadefoots can survive even if they lose nearly 50 percent of their mass to dehydration. The rains of spring and summer will bring them out for a frenzy of breeding. Without sufficient rain, the toads may not emerge, instead remaining underground until the next year. Those without sufficient stored energy cannot survive two successive seasons of hibernation, but some may make it through, emerging the next spring after not seeing the sky or breathing fresh air for nearly two years.

Great Basin Spadefoot
Spea intermontana

Field ID: Stout, small toad. Olive to gray-green with pale belly and pale stripes along sides. Fairly smooth skin with some very small warts, a lump between the eyes (farther back than on the plains spadefoot), and a hard, wedge-shaped spade on each hind foot. Eyes have vertical pupils. **Size:** 1½–2 inches (3.8–5 cm).

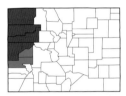

Habitat: Piñon-juniper woodlands, sagebrush grasslands, and shrublands.

Distribution: Northwestern to north central Colorado, up to about 7,000 feet.

Field Notes: Adapted to dry western shrublands, much like the plains spadefoot of the Eastern Plains the Great Basin spadefoot emerges from its hibernaculum when heavy rains fall in spring. It is active from May through September, depending on rainfall, breeding in temporary pools formed by rains and spring flooding. The male's call is a low-pitched, throaty stutter. Eggs hatch in two days, but tadpoles may not metamorphose for several weeks. These toads are nocturnal and may become inactive during very dry periods. They use the spade on their hind foot to dig burrows in loose soil.

Legal Status: Nongame.

Mexican Spadefoot/New Mexico Spadefoot
Spea multiplicata

Field ID: Gray or pale brown toad with scattered dark spots. Has a hard spade on each hind foot but lacks a lump between the eyes, which have vertical pupils. The male has a dark throat. **Size:** Up to about 2½ inches (6.4 cm).

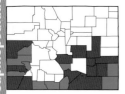

Habitat: Plains grasslands, floodplains of sagebrush grasslands, and semidesert shrublands.

Distribution: Southeastern Colorado and far southwestern Colorado, up to about 6,500 feet.

Field Notes: Like other spadefoot toads, these animals live in dry habitats and their activity is tied to spring and summer rains. They spend much of their adult life buried in the soil in order to survive dry or cold conditions. They may use the existing burrows of other animals. They emerge from hibernacula for breeding and are active May through September. Most breeding occurs in June and July. The male's breeding call is a croaking stutter or trill about one second long. Though not broadly distributed, they can be abundant in the areas where they are found. Formerly named New Mexico spadefoot.

Legal Status: Nongame.

Family Bufonidae – True Toads

This large family of toads is distributed worldwide and embodies the popular concept of what a toad is. True toads have thick, warty skin; plump, tubby bodies; and short legs. They are nocturnal and move by hopping. They lack teeth. Behind each eye they have a bump called a parotoid gland. Many also have cranial crests—ridges behind and between the eyes.

True toads have several defensive adaptations. If handled, they release fluid from their cloaca. When threatened by a predator, they fill their lungs with air, making their puffed-up bodies difficult to grab and swallow. The warts and glands that mark their skin contain poisons that cause a predator's mouth and throat to swell and can cause nausea, heart palpitations, and sometimes, death. The predator that gets a mouthful of these nasty-tasting secretions learns not to grab a toad again.

Contrary to folklore, touching toads does not cause warts.

Boreal Toad/Mountain Toad/Western Toad
Anaxyrus boreas boreas

Field ID: Medium-sized gray-green toad with dark, mottled patches. Warty skin. Pale stripe down middle of back. Warts may be reddish surrounded by black blotches. Parotoid glands are oval. Cranial crests lacking. Pattern of black blotches on a light background usually on belly. **Size:** 2½–4 inches (6.4–10 cm).

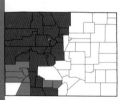

Habitat: Mountain wetlands, wet meadows, streams, beaver ponds, glacial tarns, and subalpine lakes.

Distribution: Through the central mountains of the state, usually from 8,500 to 12,000 feet.

Field Notes: Once very common and found throughout the mountains of the state, the boreal toad has disappeared from much of its former range. Hundreds of ponds and wetlands where the toads were once common now have none. An infectious fungus appears to be the main culprit. Water pollution from mine runoff and destruction and degradation of habitat due to the impact of roads, livestock grazing, logging, water management, and other activities in fragile mountain habitats probably also contribute. The Colorado Division of Wildlife (CDOW) is working on recovering this species using techniques including captive breeding and reintroduction. Sightings of boreal toads should be reported to the CDOW, including details of location. This animal is also known as the mountain or western toad.

Boreal toads become active as mountain snowpack melts, usually in May or June, and return to hibernacula as cold weather returns in September or so. Unlike most toads, they are usually silent during breeding. Males make a "release call," which sounds like the peeping of baby chicks, when grasped by another male. Most metamorphosis happens in August and September.

Legal Status: Endangered.

Amphibians in the Coal Mine

The highly absorbent skin of amphibians makes them very vulnerable to environmental pollutants and toxins in water. Like the canaries in the coal mine that miners used to warn them of poisonous gases, amphibians may be an early warning system for declines in the health of the environment. The loss or serious decline of amphibians would remove a significant component of many natural communities, impacting the environment in ways that may be difficult to predict. And when amphibians die in unusually high numbers or develop a high number of physical deformities, it may signal the presence of something in the environment that could harm humans.

Great Plains Toad
Anaxyrus cognatus

Field ID: A large, olive green, gray, or brown warty-skinned toad. Light stripe down middle of back. Pattern of large, dark blotches with light borders is symmetrical on either side of midline. Prominent bony ridges on head meet to form a hard bump on snout. Parotoid glands are large and oval. **Size:** 2–4½ inches (5–11.4 cm).

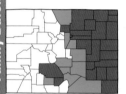

Habitat: Shortgrass and sandhills prairie, agricultural land, semidesert shrublands.

Distribution: Throughout eastern Colorado from the plains to the foothills, up to about 6,000 feet; in the San Luis Valley between 7,500 and 8,000 feet.

Field Notes: This large toad is active mainly at night from May to September, though it can also be active on cloudy, rainy days. The male's breeding call is a series of jackhammerlike pulses. Eastern Plains reservoirs with fluctuating water levels and ponds that form with spring rains make up the primary breeding areas. Seasonal precipitation is so important that in years of no rain, these toads don't breed. Though widespread in eastern Colorado, populations of Great Plains toads are localized and not abundant.

Legal Status: Nongame.

Green Toad
Anaxyrus debilis

Field ID: Small, bright green toad with black spots and irregular lines on back. Numerous small warts and large, kidney-shaped parotoid glands. Head and body are noticeably flatter than those of other toads. **Size:** 1¼–2⅛ inches (3.2–5.4 cm).

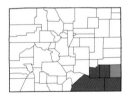

Habitat: Shortgrass prairie.

Distribution: In canyon bottoms and rolling prairie of southeastern Colorado.

Field Notes: Green toads are active from May through September. The heavy rains of late spring trigger breeding in temporary ponds and in pools formed by intermittent streams. In years when rains come late in the season, breeding may occur as late as August. The male's breeding song is a cricketlike buzz or trill lasting for up to eight seconds. Green toads are not widespread or abundant in Colorado and have been seen in just a few sites. The green toad's flattened shape allows it to squeeze into small crevices for shelter. When threatened, green toads flatten to the ground.

Legal Status: Nongame.

Red-spotted Toad
Anaxyrus punctatus

Field ID: This small toad is grayish brown to olive with tiny red warts and round, red to dark orange parotoid glands. Head and body are somewhat flattened. **Size:** 1½–3 inches (3.8–7.6 cm).

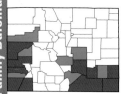

Habitat: Rocky canyons, canyon bottoms, streams in grasslands.

Distribution: Southeastern Colorado mostly south of the Arkansas River; southwestern Colorado south of the Colorado River; up to about 7,000 feet.

Field Notes: This canyon-dwelling toad lives in rugged country in the southeastern and southwestern corners of the state. Red-spotted toads breed between mid-May and August. The male's song is a high-pitched trill. It calls during the day from a hiding place in a rock crevice near its breeding pond. At night, it may call while sitting exposed on bare rock next to its pond. Because of the ephemeral nature of the toad's temporary breeding ponds, many larvae die before metamorphosing because their habitat dries up. Eggs and larvae are sometimes killed when washed out of breeding pools by canyon flash floods.

Legal Status: Nongame.

Woodhouse's Toad
Anaxyrus woodhousii

Field ID: Large toad ranging in color from yellow-brown to olive to gray, with dark, irregular mottling and dark spots. Pale stripe along middle of back. Pale belly lacking much dark patterning. Some toads have dark spots on upper chest. Warty skin. Parotoid glands are elongated. Bony ridges on head.
Size: 2½–5 inches (6.4–12.7 cm).

Habitat: Areas with sandy soil, including agricultural areas and cattle pastures; along streams, ponds, irrigation ditches, stock ponds, and temporary pools, and in canyons.

Distribution: Throughout eastern Colorado, up to about 7,000 feet; through much of western Colorado, up to about 6,000 feet; in the San Luis Valley, up to 8,000 feet.

Field Notes: This widespread and abundant toad is probably the one Coloradans are most likely to encounter. Rains in April and May cause them to emerge from hibernacula. They are mainly nocturnal, and thousands are killed by vehicles as they migrate across roads at night while attempting to reach their breeding ponds. They breed in shallow water from April through June and stay active until September or October.

They spend the hot parts of the day hidden in cool, damp places: under logs and rocks, in burrows, or beneath vegetation. The male's call is a drawn-out *wahh*, like the bawl of a calf.

Legal Status: Nongame species. Up to four individuals can be taken and possessed without a license for noncommercial purposes, though no more than 12 individuals in total of all animals from the list of allowed species can be possessed at any one time.

Frog or Toad?

Technically, there is no difference between frogs and toads. These are common names, and their use can be confusing. The canyon treefrog, for example, is plump and toadlike in appearance. Still, there are characteristics commonly associated with frogs and toads. Animals we call frogs usually have smooth, moist skin, more streamlined bodies, live in or near water, and leap rather than hop. Toads have warty skin, chunky bodies, live on land or in drier habitats, and move by hopping.

Family Microhylidae – Narrow-mouthed Toads

Narrow-mouthed toads are shy and nocturnal. Because of their secretive habits, they are rarely seen. They spend much of their lives underground in burrows or among rocks.

The bodies of narrow-mouthed toads are plump. Their narrow shoulders and head and pointed muzzle give them a teardrop shape. They have short, stout legs and a fold of skin across the back of the head. The skin is moist and smooth. Narrow-mouthed toads lack teeth. Ants are their primary food.

This family is found in the Americas, Asia, Africa, Australia, and New Guinea.

Western Narrow-mouthed Toad
Gastrophryne olivacea

Field ID: Tiny, smooth-skinned, gray or brown toad with black flecks. Plump body and small head with pointed snout. Fold of skin across back of head. **Size:** $7/8$–$1\,5/8$ inches (2.2–4.1 cm).

Habitat: Rocky canyon slopes and bottoms; edges of temporary pools and stock ponds.

Distribution: Southeastern corner of the state.

Field Notes: Narrow-mouthed toads are secretive and active at night. They feed primarily on ants. The male's breeding song is a high-pitched, buzzing bleat that lasts up to four seconds and is often preceded by a brief whistle. Narrow-mouthed toads are not common in Colorado and have only been found north of the Oklahoma border along the Baca–Las Animas county line. They were first described in the state in 1979. These toads are active between May and August, mainly after a rain. They are very tolerant of high temperatures. Studies in other states have found that narrow-mouthed toads often share burrows with tarantulas, which are not uncommon in southeastern Colorado. The tarantulas may protect the toads from predators, while the toads eat ants that might bother the tarantula, its eggs, and young.

Legal Status: Species of special concern.

Family Hylidae – Treefrogs

Treefrogs are small, slender-bodied frogs with long, slim legs. They climb and walk but rarely hop. Some species live on the ground, but most are tree-dwellers. They have special pads on the tips of their toes that act like little suction cups, helping them stick to vertical surfaces as they climb. Cartilage separating the last two bones of each toe makes the toes flexible so that a climbing frog can swivel and change direction while the toe pads stay stuck to the surface, securely in place. The pupils of their eyes are horizontal. During the breeding season, treefrogs call from perches over, near, or in water.

This is a large family with nearly 900 species distributed through the Americas, Europe, Asia, and northern Africa.

Northern Cricket Frog
Acris crepitans

Field ID: Tiny, smooth-skinned, grayish or tan frog with dark spots and marks. Large, dark triangle between eyes. Dark stripe running down back of each thigh. Extensive webbing between toes of each hind foot. **Size:** ⅝–1¼ inches (1.6–3.2 cm).

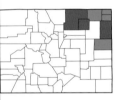

Habitat: Sunny, marshy edges of waterways, including ponds, reservoirs, ditches, and streams.

Distribution: Northeastern Colorado along the north and south forks of the Republican River; possibly along the South Platte River drainage in Weld and Morgan counties.

Field Notes: Biologists are uncertain whether northern cricket frogs still survive in Colorado. They were found in the Republican River drainage in northeastern Colorado through the 1970s, but the last known sighting was in 1979. If you see a cricket frog, try to take a picture, note your location, and report your sighting to the Colorado Division of Wildlife. Cricket frogs are active from April through October, depending on the arrival of warm weather. The voice of the breeding male is a distinctive clicking, like two stones being tapped together—*ti, ti.* When alarmed, cricket frogs quickly leap into water and hide under vegetation, but will soon emerge if there is no further disturbance.

Legal Status: Species of special concern.

Canyon Treefrog
Hyla arenicolor

Field ID: Plump and toadlike. Light brown to gray, with darker blotches. Back of thighs and groin are yellowish orange. Toes have rounded pads. Hind feet are webbed, but webbing does not extend to the top of fifth toe. **Size:** 1¼–2¼ inches (3.2–5.7 cm).

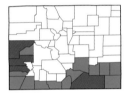

Habitat: Intermittent and seasonal streams in deep canyons; permanent pools along canyon bottoms.

Distribution: Western Colorado south of the Colorado River near the Utah border, at 4,500 to 6,300 feet; in eastern Colorado in Las Animas County around Mesa de Maya.

Field Notes: Sitting, this treefrog looks like a toad, with a thick body and warty skin. The male's song is a series of one-toned nasal warbles that each last one to three seconds. Treefrogs spend winter and cold periods in rock crevices. Breeding success is highly dependent on rainfall, and populations ebb and flow depending on annual precipitation. Treefrogs are not easy to find. They live in remote canyons, where they hide in rock crevices during the day, becoming active at night. Even basking in full sight on a rock, they blend in almost completely. Recent observations of treefrogs in southeastern Colorado confirmed their presence there. Previously, there had been only a single record, dating from the late 1800s.

Legal Status: Nongame.

Boreal Chorus Frog
Pseudacris maculata

Field ID: Tiny, smooth-skinned frog. Green, brown, or reddish; dark stripes and spots on back. A dark stripe extends from the snout, through each eye, and down the side. **Size:** ¾–1½ inches (1.9–3.8 cm).

Habitat: Around ponds, wetlands, wet meadows, drainage catchments, runoff ponds, meadows with seasonal puddles, and backwaters of streams.

Distribution: Throughout much of the state, up to about 12,000 feet; uncommon in southeastern and central western Colorado.

Field Notes: This small, common frog adapts well to a variety of habitats in the state, from eastern prairies to mountain wetlands to suburban storm drainage ponds. Its characteristic song—like someone running a thumb down a comb, rising in pitch—can be heard throughout spring and summer, even from a long distance away. Chorus frogs emerge from hibernacula as early as March in lower elevations and remain active until September or October, sometimes even after the first snowfall. They are active during the day and into evening and night during the breeding season. Those found at lower elevations are small, about the size of a dime, but animals in high mountain areas can get quite large, up to 1½ inches (3.8 cm).

Legal Status: Nongame species. Up to four individuals can be taken and possessed without a license for noncommercial purposes, though no more than 12 individuals in total of all animals from the list of allowed species can be possessed at any one time.

A Little Night Music

On summer evenings in Colorado, the breeding calls of male frogs and toads enliven the Colorado outdoors with music (of a sort). The calls are so distinctive that many species can be identified by sound. Some of the more familiar include:

- Plains spadefoot—a brief, distinct grating sound, almost like the quack of a duck
- Woodhouse's toad—a loud, nasal *waaah*
- Boreal chorus frog—like someone running a thumb down a comb, rising in pitch
- Northern leopard frog—a low sound like a motorboat, mixed with grunts and chuckles
- Bullfrog—a deep, resonant croak that sounds like *jug-o-rum*

Only the boreal toad (also called mountain or western toad) does not have a loud breeding call, because males lack an inflatable vocal sac. Visit the *Colorado Herpetofaunal Atlas* online to hear recordings of amphibian calls—http://ndis.nrel.colostate.edu/herpatlas/coherpatlas.

Family Ranidae – True Frogs

This large family includes the animals that are the most common image of a frog in the public perception. They are found over most of the world, on all continents except Antarctica. Those inhabiting North America have long legs with pointed toes and webbed hind feet. Their skin is smooth and moist. They are carnivorous and live in, or mostly in, water, where they hunt insects and other prey. With their long, strong legs, true frogs are jumpers rather than hoppers (like toads). The pupils of their eyes are horizontal, and they have teeth only in the upper jaw.

Spring ushers in the classic time of frog courtship and mating, when groups of males fill ponds and sing loudly to attract females.

Plains Leopard Frog
Lithobates blairi

Field ID: Medium-large brown to tan frog with darker round or oval spots that often have pale edges. Dark striping on backs of hind legs. Skin is somewhat rough and warty, with folds along the sides of the back that are broken and inset at the waist. Hind toes are webbed. Pale stripe along jaw. A light spot is often visible on the eardrum. **Size:** 2–4³⁄₈ inches (5–11.1 cm).

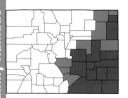

Habitat: Edges of streams, ponds, ditches, and pools; in grasslands; and at canyon bottoms.

Distribution: In southeastern Colorado in the Arkansas River basin; in the Republican River basin in northeastern Colorado; up to about 5,000 feet.

Field Notes: Leopard frogs emerge from wintering sites in late March or April and remain active through October. During the warm months, they are active in the day and night. The male's breeding song is a series of guttural, chuckling notes. In fall, leopard frogs may migrate in great numbers to certain ponds where they will spend the winter burrowed into the leaves or mud at the bottom of the pond. Leopard frog populations are being affected by the presence of nonnative bullfrogs, which eat leopard frog eggs, larvae, and adults. In some areas, especially where bullfrogs are present, leopard frogs have disappeared from ponds where they were once common.

Legal Status: Species of special concern.

American Bullfrog
Lithobates catesbeianus

Field ID: Very large green or brown frog with dark spots or mottling and a pale belly. Throat of male is yellow during breeding season. Hind feet are fully webbed except for the last joint of the longest toe. Large, external eardrums. **Size:** 3½–8 inches (8.9–20.3 cm).

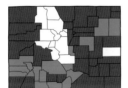

Habitat: Reservoirs, permanent ponds and pools; slow-flowing streams and ditches with cattails and emergent vegetation.

Distribution: Along the South Platte and Arkansas river drainages of eastern Colorado; along the Colorado River and in scattered western Colorado locations; in the San Luis Valley.

Field Notes: The bullfrog is the classic frog of popular perception. It is the largest frog in North America, its *jug-o-rum* call punctuating summer nights around ponds in rural areas and even cities. Bullfrogs usually remain close to water. They are not native to Colorado, but have become well-established along river drainages of eastern Colorado and along the Colorado River in western Colorado. How they were introduced is uncertain—probably accidentally through stocking of fish and intentionally in some areas by locals who wanted to establish populations for hunting. Bullfrogs are large, voracious predators and are linked to the decline of native species such as northern and plains leopard frogs. They may live up to 10 years in the wild.

Legal Status: Game species. An unlimited number of bullfrogs may be collected or possessed year-round with a valid fishing license.

Northern Leopard Frog
Lithobates pipiens

Field ID: Medium-large green or brownish frog. Dark round or oval spots; dark striping on the backs of the hind legs; pale stripe along jaw. Skin is fairly smooth, with folds along the sides of the back that are not inset or broken at the waist. Hind toes are webbed. **Size:** 2–5 inches (5–12.7 cm).

Habitat: Wet meadows and the grassy banks and edges of ponds, marshes, streams, and ditches.

Distribution: Statewide, up to about 11,000 feet, except in the southeastern and east-central parts of the state.

Field Notes: The leopard frog nicely fits the popular perception of a frog, with its smooth, greenish skin and perpetual smile. It likes the grass in wet meadows and at the edges of ponds, and if startled will zigzag away in great leaps until it hits the water with a splash. An adult frog can jump as far as 3 feet. Leopard frogs emerge in March and April at lower elevations (later at higher elevations) and are active day and night. The male's song is a low snore lasting about three seconds, followed by clucking notes. Leopard frogs have disappeared from or become much less numerous at many sites where they were once abundant. Biologists are concerned that in addition to taking over or degrading habitat, nonnative bullfrogs may be reducing northern leopard frog populations in many areas. Bullfrogs metamorphose earlier than leopard frogs, eat leopard frog larvae and adults, and may carry diseases, such as the amphibian chytrid fungus, to native frogs.

Legal Status: Species of special concern.

Wood Frog
Lithobates sylvaticus

Field ID: Small, fairly smooth-skinned gray to brown frog. Prominent dark mask through eyes and on either side of face that extends to the corner of the jaw. Hind toes are webbed. Folds along sides of back. Often has a pale stripe down center of back. **Size:** 1⅜–3¼ inches (3.5–8.3 cm).

Habitat: Mountain ponds, lakes, wet meadows, stream edges, and subalpine marshes and bogs.

Distribution: North-central Colorado around North Park; tributary streams around the headwaters of the Colorado River and the upper end of the Laramie River; between about 8,200 and 9,800 feet.

Field Notes: This hardy frog is found clear up into Alaska—farther north in North America than any other amphibian—so it is understandable that in Colorado wood frogs dwell in mountain habitats up to almost 10,000 feet. Wood frogs emerge from hibernacula in May and are active day and night through summer. The mountain breeding season is necessarily short, sometimes one week or less, and during this time, breeding adults do not feed. The male's song is a series of short, rasping, quacklike notes. The frogs return to winter hibernacula in September. The wood frog's body chemistry allows it to survive partial freezing. Despite earlier concerns, wood frog populations in Colorado seem to be stable, though distribution is very limited.

Legal Status: Species of special concern.

I'm Simply Freezing!

Wood and chorus frogs can literally freeze and live to tell about it. Both of these species can tolerate the formation of ice within their tissues. As the animal begins to freeze, glucose, which lowers the freezing temperature of liquids, floods the body from the liver. Water moves out of the tissues, so most of the ice forms between organs, minimizing damage. Because glucose is highest at the body's core, frogs actually thaw from the inside out. The heart keeps beating as long as it can, then, upon thawing, resumes beating while parts of the frog are still frozen. Glucose is excreted into the bladder, then is reabsorbed as an energy source.

REPTILES
CLASS REPTILIA

What Is a Reptile?

From turtles encased in armored shells to wall-climbing lizards to snakes that can swim and climb trees without arms or legs, reptiles are a fascinating group of animals. They are categorized by biologists as part of the class Reptilia. Reptiles evolved from amphibians some 300 million years ago. While amphibians are tied to aquatic habitats, the development of protective body scales, eggs encased in hard or leathery shells, and larger, more efficient lungs allowed reptiles to move away from water and live their entire life cycle on land. Adapting to a variety of terrestrial habitats, reptiles became extremely diverse.

Many reptiles are well-adapted to life in arid, rocky habitats, and are much more abundant in our state than amphibians. Colorado is home to 28 species of snakes, 17 species of lizards, and 6 species of turtles. In general, reptiles are not high-altitude animals, and few live above 6,000 feet. The highest-altitude reptile in Colorado, the terrestrial gartersnake, lives at up to 11,000 feet and has even been found above 13,000 feet.

Characteristics of Reptiles

Reptiles are air-breathing and do not lay their eggs in water. Many are well-adapted to dry habitats. They have dry, scaly skin and claws on their toes. Most reptiles have a three-chambered heart.

Reptiles are ectothermic, or cold blooded, meaning they derive body heat from the environment rather than generating it internally, as mammals and birds do. They become sluggish in cool weather and usually bask in the sun to warm their bodies and become active. Many hibernate in winter, though some become active on warm, sunny days.

Reptiles practice internal fertilization. They lay eggs or bear live young, and the embryo develops inside a fluid-filled sac, the amnion, which keeps it from drying out. Turtles lay hard-shelled eggs (though not as hard as a bird egg). Lizards and snakes lay leathery-skinned eggs. Some reptiles, such as the northern watersnake, bear live young. The young develop within a membranous sac within the female's body and are not nurtured through a placenta, as with mammals. Other snakes, including rattlesnakes, do something in between—the female retains the eggs within her body, they hatch inside her, and the hatched young are then born.

Though all grouped within one class, reptiles, with such a variety of physical adaptations, are a very diverse group of animals.

TURTLES: ORDER TESTUDINES

The members of this order won't be mistaken for any other creatures. Despite variation in design, appearance, and lifestyle, they are all turtles, and all have shells.

The turtle's shell isn't an outer skeleton (like the exoskeleton of an insect) but is made from the fusing of numerous bones of the back and rib cage. Despite cartoons to the contrary, the shell can't be taken off like an overcoat. The chest and pelvic girdles are located within the rib cage, a skeletal arrangement unique to turtles. The legs are short and extremely side-slung as a modification to accommodate the shell.

Turtles are classified in two suborders based on the method used to retract the head. In suborder Peurodira, the neck bones flex to the side, allowing the head to be pulled in sideways. In suborder Cryptodires, which includes all Colorado turtles, the neck bones flex vertically so the head is drawn straight back into the shell.

Family Chelydridae – Snapping Turtles

Snapping turtles are large turtles with massive heads, long tails, and thick, strong legs with heavy claws. They have strong jaws and hooked beaks. Their shells are small for their body size, particularly the plastron, and the carapace has 12 scutes along each side.

These primitive-looking turtles spend their lives in water, usually submerged at the bottom of a still pond. They have lungs, not gills, so they must surface to breathe but can tolerate long periods with little oxygen. They feed on whatever they find or can catch.

This is a New World family, with just two species in North America. Only the snapping turtle inhabits Colorado. The alligator snapping turtle of the southeastern United States can grow to more than 200 pounds and has a pink wormlike appendage on its tongue that it uses like a lure to attract prey.

Snapping Turtle
Chelydra serpentina

Field ID: Very large, grayish brown to dark brown turtle. Hard shell, large head with a hooked beak, heavy legs, webbed toes, and powerful claws. Carapace has a saw-toothed rear edge. Tail is as long or longer than carapace, with a ridge of large, bony scales along its top. Adult's carapace is mostly smooth. Juvenile's has three ridges running from front to back. Small plastron is not hinged. **Size:** 8–19½ inches (20.3–49.5 cm).

Habitat: Permanent streams, ponds, and reservoirs with silty, muddy bottoms, especially those with submerged logs and vegetation.

Distribution: Eastern Colorado along the Arkansas, South Platte, and Republican river drainages; up to about 5,500 feet.

Field Notes: Snapping turtles spend most of their time submerged at the bottom of ponds and waterways, moving through the mud. When they surface, their shells are often crusted with mud and algae. In cooler weather, they bask in the sun on emergent logs or by floating at the surface. They are active from about March to October, hibernating in winter buried in the mud at the bottom of ponds or beneath submerged logs or overhangs. During hibernation, their metabolism is greatly reduced and they tolerate very low oxygen levels and live on stored body fat. After emerging, they may migrate overland to nesting sites or from a drying pond to new habitat. Snapping turtles will snap aggressively with their sharp beaks if handled and can injure people, pets, and livestock.

Legal Status: Game species. An unlimited number of snapping turtles can be taken between April 1 and October 31 with a valid small-game or fishing license. Private landowners can kill "snappers" without a license if they are damaging crops, property, or livestock.

An RV on Legs

A turtle's shell is sort of like an RV the animal moves around and lives in, but never gets out of. Children's stories notwithstanding, a turtle is not able to slip out of its shell, nor is the shell ever shed. The shell is formed from vertebrae, ribs, and other bones that have modified and fused. It is living tissue that grows with the turtle. Because the shell has a blood and nerve supply, if it is injured or cut, it can bleed and cause the animal pain, and the shell may show scars. This bony structure is covered by horny, protective plates called scutes. The scutes are made of keratin, the same material fingernails are made of. The fused seams between the scutes give the shell its geometric pattern.

Family Emydidae – Pond and Box Turtles

This is the largest family of turtles and includes most turtle species in the United States. In Colorado it includes two native turtles and one introduced species. Most of this family have flattened, low-profile shells and live in or near water, but box turtles have high, domed shells and live on land. The head and neck are smooth, and the shell is covered with scutes. The hind feet are flat and partly webbed.

Aquatic species often climb out of the water onto a log or bank and bask in the sun. Some species have elaborate courtship behaviors in which the male strokes the female's head with his claws.

Painted Turtle
Chrysemys picta

Field ID: Medium to large turtle. Olive to dark green or black; hard, somewhat smooth shell with a pattern of narrow yellow lines between the scutes. Plastron is orange to reddish with dark marks and may be intricately patterned. Head, neck, and legs are green with yellow stripes. **Size:** 4–9½ inches (10.2–24.1 cm).

Habitat: Lakes, ponds, and slow-moving waterways, especially those with silty bottoms, thick vegetation, and submerged logs.

Distribution: Eastern Plains and the Front Range, up to 6,000 feet; in the southwest corner of the state, up to 8,500 feet.

Field Notes: Painted turtles can often be seen basking in the sun on logs and pond banks. They often trail one leg in the water. Sometimes dozens of turtles will crowd onto a favorite log, and they may become aggressive with each other. Turtles floating in the water will poke their heads up like periscopes, ducking underwater again if they feel threatened. Painted turtles spend the winter burrowed into the mud at the bottom of ponds, emerging in March or April and staying active through mid-November. Hibernating turtles have a greatly reduced metabolism, so they need very little oxygen. Male turtles mature in about three years, females in eight to ten years. They may live as long as 40 years. Painted turtles are the most widely distributed turtle in North America. In 2008, the painted turtle became Colorado's official state reptile.

Legal Status: Nongame species. Up to four individuals can be taken and possessed without a license for noncommercial purposes, though no more than 12 individuals in total of all animals from the list of allowed species can be possessed at any one time.

Red-eared Slider/Pond Slider
Trachemys scripta elegans

Field ID: Medium to large turtle. Greenish to olive. Oval cara-pace is weakly keeled with a distinctive pattern of yellow bars, stripes, and spots. Plastron is yellow and may be plain or intricately patterned. Prominent red, orange, or yellow stripe on each side of the face behind the eye. Yellow streaks running down the face, neck, and legs. **Size:** 5–11⅝ inches (12.7–29.5 cm).

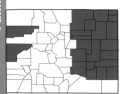

Habitat: Lakes, ponds, and sluggish streams and waterways; prefers those with silty bottoms, thick vegetation, and submerged logs.

Distribution: Believed to be in many areas of the Eastern Plains and the Front Range, especially in urban and suburban parks and open spaces, as well as in western Colorado, especially in Mesa and Rio Blanco coun-ties; up to 6,000 feet.

Field Notes: This nonnative turtle is a popular dime store pet, and millions of them have been raised on turtle farms and sold commercially, though few survive to adulthood.

These ubiquitous pets are reportedly now found on every continent except Antarctica. The species has become established in Colorado from the release of unwanted pets into ponds and wetlands. Though well-intentioned, the introduction of non-native species is not good for native wildlife. Exotic animals compete with natives for food, shelter, and living space, and may introduce diseases and parasites. Sliders love to bask in the sun and can be found piled atop one another on favorite logs and banks. They begin life as tiny turtles the size of a quarter but can grow to the size of a dinner plate. Younger turtles feed on aquatic insects, invertebrates, and tadpoles, turning to aquatic plants, algae, and other vegetation as they mature. The red-eared slider is a subspecies of pond slider.

Legal Status: Unregulated. May be imported, sold, bartered, traded, transferred, possessed, propagated, and transported in Colorado.

Ornate Box Turtle
Terrapene ornata

Field ID: This terrestrial turtle has a hard, domed brown or black shell with an intricate pattern of yellow lines. Plastron also has a yellow pattern and a yellow line down the center, as well as a distinct single hinge. Male: Red eyes. Female: Yellowish brown eyes. **Size:** 4–5¾ inches (10.2–14.6 cm).

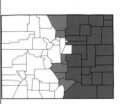

Habitat: Shortgrass and sandhills prairie.

Distribution: Throughout eastern Colorado, up to about 5,500 feet.

Field Notes: With its domed, patterned shell and lumbering gait, the box turtle is the classic turtle of dry western landscapes. It finds good habitat throughout the eastern prairies, where there is soft soil it can burrow into to escape daytime heat. Box turtles are often taken home as pets, but removing them from their native habitat can be a death sentence. Because of their low reproductive rate, it also potentially hurts the species. Thousands of turtles are run over every year while crossing roads. Box turtles are active from late April through October. The hinged lower shell allows the box turtle to pull in its head and "shut the door," closing the forward portion of the plastron against the carapace.

Legal Status: Nongame species. Up to four individuals can be taken and possessed without a license for noncommercial purposes, though no more than 12 individuals in total of all animals from the list of allowed species can be possessed at any one time.

Family Kinosternidae – Mud and Musk Turtles

These aquatic turtles are well-named, spending much of their lives buried in the soft mud of still ponds. They have musk glands beneath the carapace that produce strong-smelling secretions. The strong smell has led to nicknames such as "stinkpot" or "stinking Jim."

Turtles of this family have a small, smooth carapace with 11 scutes around the edges on each side. The rear of the carapace lacks serrations. The plastron is single or double hinged and has 10 or 11 scutes. Males have a long tail with a hard, horny nail at the tip while the female's tail is short.

Unlike pond turtles, which like to crawl out of the water and bask in the sun, members of this family float at the surface in still water or among pond vegetation, with just the back of the shell visible above water. Researchers recently discovered that the common musk turtle, a species not found in Colorado, has a specially adapted tongue that can extract oxygen from water, allowing it to stay submerged for long periods.

Yellow Mud Turtle
Kinosternon flavescens

Field ID: The yellow mud turtle is actually brown or olive, with a smooth, hard, oval shell that is often coated with algae. The tail is long and thick, with spines on the tip. All four feet are webbed. Plastron is hinged at the front and back. **Size:** 3½–6⅜ inches (8.9–16.2 cm).

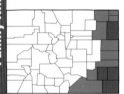

Habitat: Permanent and intermittent ponds, streams, pools, ditches, and flooded fields, as well as nearby grass-lands and sandhills.

Distribution: Eastern Colorado below 5,000 feet in the Republican, Arkansas, and Cimarron river drainages.

Field Notes: *Mud turtle* is a good name for this animal, which spends much of its time in the water, evidenced by the frequent growth of algae on its shell. When a seasonal pond inhabited by mud turtles dries up, the turtles will move onto land and migrate to new, permanent ponds. Females lay their eggs in the sand or soil away from water. Mud turtles are active from April through October, but in midsummer will estivate (become inactive during hot weather) for a time. The plastron is double-hinged, so the mud turtle can "close up shop" on both ends when threatened.

Legal Status: Species of special concern.

Turtle, Tortoise, or Terrapin?

Like *frog* and *toad*, the words *turtle*, *tortoise*, and *terrapin* are common rather than technical terms, and their meanings vary in different locations and countries. The term *turtle* applies to all members of the family. Large turtles that live on land are often called tortoises. Most tortoises have high, domed shells that make it difficult for predators to grasp them. Aquatic turtles have smooth, flattened, streamlined shells that help them glide through water. Terrapins are usually semiaquatic, though they can be fresh- or saltwater dwelling. *Terrapin* is not used as a common name for any turtles native to Colorado.

Family Trionychidae – Softshell Turtles

This is a family of highly aquatic turtles. They have very long necks with small heads and pronounced nostrils at the tip of the snout. This allows them to remain submerged with only the snorkel-like nose extended above the surface to breathe. They are strong swimmers and motor along beneath the water, breathing through their "snorkels." They will emerge to bask near the edge of the water, but escape quickly back into the water if frightened. If handled, they can whip their long necks around to deliver a fierce bite with strong jaws.

Softshell turtles have an oval or round, flattened carapace covered with soft, leathery skin rather than hard scutes. Their webbed feet are flat and paddlelike, and have three claws. Females are much larger than males, and their carapaces develop a mottled pattern.

Spiny Softshell
Apalone spinifera

Field ID: Medium-sized turtle with a flattened, oval shell. Shell is smooth, soft, and flexible, covered with a leathery skin instead of the hard, horny scutes of most turtles. Carapace is olive to gray to tan, with black-bordered dark blotches and a dark line around the edge. Leading edge has a line of spiny knobs. Small head, long neck, and snorkel-like nose. Feet are paddlelike and fully webbed, with three claws on the front feet. **Size:** 5–9¼ inches (12.7–23.5 cm).

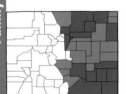

Habitat: Rivers, streams, intermittent streams, and adjacent ponds; prefers waterways with a soft, silty, or sandy bottom.

Distribution: Eastern Colorado below 5,500 feet, along the South Platte, Republican, Arkansas, and Cimarron river drainages.

Field Notes: Primarily an aquatic turtle, the softshell is wonderfully adapted to its life in the water. Floating or swimming just below the surface, it extends its long neck and pokes its snout above the water like a snorkel to breathe. Its gas-permeable skin also absorbs oxygen from the water, increasing the time the turtle can spend submerged. Its paddle-shaped feet are adapted for swimming. Softshells are active during the day from April through October, burying themselves in the sand or mud to sleep at night. They are wary animals and will claw and scratch if handled. They have been reported to shoot blood from their eyes as a defensive behavior.

Legal Status: Nongame.

LIZARDS: ORDER SQUAMATA, SUBORDER LACERTILIA

Order Squamata, which includes lizards and snakes, is the largest and most diverse order of reptiles, with some 7,000 species. The bodies of these animals are covered with scales, and they all occasionally shed their skin.

Suborder Lacertilia is made up of the lizards, with close to 5,000 species. This large group is found on all continents except Antarctica. Lizards range in size from tiny chameleons only an inch or two long to the nine-foot-long Komodo dragon. Most have four limbs, external ears, eardrums, moveable eyelids, and a fleshy tongue. These characteristics separate them from the snakes, which belong to the same order but a different suborder (Serpentes).

Lizards generally have long bodies and tails. Many have fracture zones of cartilage or connective tissue within the tail. If a predator traps the lizard by the tail, the tail pulls away and the lizard escapes. The tail then regenerates, though it is usually shorter, colored differently, and made of cartilage rather than bone. Lizards see well, have color vision, and often have bright body colors. They communicate with body posture and movements, body color, and chemical signals.

Note: Measurements for lizards are for total length (TL) from tip of nose to tip of tail.

Family Crotaphytidae –
Collared and Leopard Lizards

This is a family of arid-country lizards found in the south-western United States and northern Mexico. They have long bodies and legs; large, distinctive heads; well-defined necks; very long tails; and strongly colored and patterned bodies. Extremely quick, they dart around their canyon and desert habitat in pursuit of prey or to elude predators. They are diurnal and carnivorous, often feeding on other lizards as well as insects and invertebrates. When running, they are able to rise up and move on their hind legs, sprinting at up to 16 miles per hour. This group of lizards is known to make a squealing vocalization when disturbed.

Eastern Collared Lizard
Crotaphytus collaris

Field ID: Large-headed, long-tailed, yellowish brown to bluish green lizard. Conspicuous black-and-white collar across back of neck. Head is sometimes a bright yellow. Pattern of light spots on back. Scales are smooth and granular. In western Colorado, toes of adults are yellow. In southeastern Colorado, male adults have yellow or orange throats; in western Colorado, their throats have dark spots or pale circles. **Size:** 8–14 inches (20.3–35.6 cm).

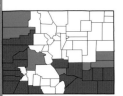

Habitat: Rocky canyons, hillsides, arroyos, shrublands, piñon-juniper woodlands.

Distribution: South of the Roan Plateau in western Colorado, up to 8,000 feet; in southeastern Colorado south of the Arkansas River, up to 7,000 feet.

Field Notes: A large collared lizard in full color—bright green body and yellow head—basking in the sun on a rock is quite a sight. The collared lizard has a more-defined head than other lizards, with a blunter snout. Adult males are very territorial and will not tolerate the intrusion of other males, particularly during the breeding season. They bob up and down aggressively and may charge and chase away competitors. If startled, a collared lizard may rise up on its hind legs, lift its tail, and run off like a mini–*Tyrannosaurus rex*. Collared lizards will bite hard if handled, and may hold on, so be cautious around them. They leap easily from rock to rock, rushing at and grabbing their prey.

Legal Status: Nongame.

Long-nosed Leopard Lizard
Gambelia wislizenii

Field ID: Large lizard; brownish gray with numerous small, dark spots and small, smooth scales. Grows darker in cooler weather. Tail is long, slender, and round (not flattened). Defined head and neck. Female: Larger than male, with orange spots and streaks on sides and neck and under tail during breeding season. **Size:** 8½–15⅛ inches (21.6–38.4 cm).

Habitat: Shrublands and mesa tops with bare ground and sparse grass.

Distribution: West-central and extreme southwestern Colorado, up to about 5,200 feet.

Field Notes: These lizards are active during the day. They may stalk their prey or lie in wait, camouflaged against the rocks, waiting for food to come to them. They can rise up and run on their hind legs, and will bite if handled. Leopard lizards have a short season of activity, emerging from hibernation in mid- to late May. Adults return underground in early August. Hatchlings, which emerge in early August, remain active through early September. They eat insects and other lizards, sometimes nearly as large as themselves.

Legal Status: Species of special concern.

Family Phrynosomatidae – Phrynosomatid Lizards

This very diverse family of lizards includes some of the most familiar and commonly seen lizards in North America, including the fence, horned, spiny, and sand lizards. Its members are found from southern Canada into Panama. Many of the species are adapted to dry habitats such as deserts, canyons, and dry grasslands. They have side-slung legs and long bodies that are round or flattened in cross section. There are fracture lines on their tails that allow the tail to break away if trapped by a predator. The tail will grow back, but shorter and different in color. Some members of this group lay eggs while others bear live young. These lizards are known for dramatic courtship and defensive displays in which they vigorously bob their heads and do "push-ups," raising their chests up and down repeatedly, often to flash dramatically colored patches of skin on throat, chest, or belly.

Common Lesser Earless Lizard
Holbrookia maculata

Field ID: Small, grayish brown lizard with a striped or spotted pattern of dark and light scales down its back. Scales are smooth and granular. Pale stripe down center and along each side of back. No external ear openings. Male: Two black marks, with blue edges, on either side of belly. Female: Black marks lack blue edges. During breeding season has yellow on sides of head and orange on sides of body. **Size:** 4–5⅛ inches (10.2–13 cm).

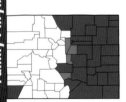

Habitat: Grasslands and shrublands with bare ground and sparse vegetation, including prairie dog towns.

Distribution: Throughout eastern Colorado, up to 6,000 feet; in the far southwestern corner of the state in Montezuma County.

Field Notes: Earless lizards are active during the day from April through October. Males court females by bobbing up and down. Females develop bright yellow or orange patches on the throat, neck, and head, and orange streaks on the sides during the breeding season. The absence of external ears may be an adaptation to these lizards' habit of burrowing headfirst into the sand. The species' body color varies with the soil color of their habitat. A subspecies inhabiting White Sands, New Mexico, the bleached earless lizard, is nearly white.

Legal Status: Nongame species. Up to four individuals can be taken and possessed without a license for noncommercial purposes, though no more than 12 individuals in total of all animals from the list of allowed species can be possessed at any one time.

In the Twitch of a Tail

A predator stalks a lizard, pounces…and is left with nothing but the lizard's twitching tail. The tails of many lizards are adapted to break away as a defense against predation. The muscles pull apart easily, and fracture zones in the tail bones give way. The blood vessels constrict so there is little blood loss. Muscles in the dropped tail continue to contract, causing the tail to twitch, distracting the predator while the lizard escapes. The tail will grow back, but out of cartilage instead of bone. The regrown tail is shorter and colored differently. The loss of its tail isn't without cost to the lizard. Tailless animals can't run as fast or defend their territories as well. They also lose an important area of fat storage in the base of the tail.

Texas Horned Lizard
Phrynosoma cornutum

Field ID: Short-tailed lizard with a wide, flattened body. Long spines on back of head are longer than they are wide. Spiky spines across the back, tail, legs, and head. Two rows of fringe-like spines along sides of body. Body is grayish brown with large, dark spots. Chest and sides have a yellow wash. Dark bars radiate from eyes. There is often a thin, pale stripe down the middle of the back. Scales on the belly are keeled. **Size:** 2½–7 inches (6.4–17.8 cm).

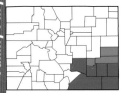

Habitat: Prairie grasslands, canyons, and mesas with sparse vegetation and areas of bare earth.

Distribution: The southeastern corner of the state, south of the Arkansas River, up to about 6,000 feet.

Field Notes: The Texas horned lizard has two distinctive long spines on the back of its head that, along with all its other spikes and body armor, give it the look of a tiny, tubby dragon. It uses the spines defensively and may try to jab a predator (or human collector) by throwing back its head. If grabbed by a predator, the lizard arches its back and neck so the spines make it difficult to swallow. The lizard may also defensively squirt blood from its eyes. The Texas horned lizard and Hernandez's short-horned lizard have contiguous ranges, which can help in species identification. Texas horned lizards are active from mid-April through late September. Harvester ants are their main food.

Legal Status: Species of special concern.

Hernandez's Short-horned Lizard
Phrynosoma hernandesi hernandesi

Field ID: Wide-bodied, short-legged lizard. Spines across back, tail, legs, and head. Spines on the back of head are as long as they are wide at the base. Body is flattened and grayish brown with black, brown, and white streaks and speckles. Some specimens have a yellow or orange wash. There is a fringe of scales along the sides of the body. **Size:** 2½–5⅞ inches (6.4–14.9 cm).

Habitat: Sagebrush and semidesert shrublands; shortgrass prairie; piñon-juniper and pine-oak woodlands; open, coniferous forests in the mountains.

Distribution: Through much of eastern, southern, and western Colorado, except for the central mountains, up to about 8,500 feet; specimens have been found above 11,000 feet in southwestern Colorado.

Field Notes: The horned lizard looks like a mini-dinosaur, with spikes and spines studding its head and body. Despite its fearsome appearance, this lizard is not aggressive, relying on its cryptic coloration and armored skin to protect it. Unlike some of its slim-bodied, darting relatives, the horned lizard is slow and lumbering, clambering through vegetation on short, side-slung legs. These lizards are hard to find, and biologists are unsure how much this is due to their effective body camouflage or to declines in population. They are active from mid-April through September, and into October at lower elevations. During courtship, both male and female bob their heads. The male may lick the female's neck and head. This is the only Colorado lizard to give birth to live young. Though horned lizards are easy to catch and seem like they'd make cute pets, they don't do well in captivity and it is illegal to possess them. Hernandez's short-horned lizard is a subspecies of greater short-horned lizard.

Legal Status: Nongame.

Round-tailed Horned Lizard
Phrynosoma modestum

Field ID: Short-legged, round-bodied lizard. Four short spines of equal length on back of head. Gray to tan or brown, depending on local soil color. Dark blotch on each side of neck. Tail is round (not flattened) and has dark bands. Body spines less prominent than on other horned lizards. Lacks a fringe of spines on the sides of its body. **Size:** 3–4¼ inches (7.6–10.8 cm).

Habitat: Dry grasslands and shrublands with open patches of sandy or gravelly soil.

Distribution: Northwestern Otero County and northeastern Las Animas County.

Field Notes: The existence of this species in Colorado is based on a handful of records. There may be other populations that haven't been discovered or reported. In Colorado, round-tailed lizards are probably active during the day from April through September or early October. Ants are their primary food. When threatened, this lizard flattens to the ground, looking like a pebble and blending in so that it is nearly impossible to see. It can shoot blood out of its eyes and may also hiss, bloat up by inhaling air, bite, kick, and elevate its horns to make it harder to swallow.

Legal Status: Species of special concern.

Common Sagebrush Lizard
Sceloporus graciosus

Field ID: Grayish to brown lizard with darker spots and bars and faint, pale stripes along the sides of its back. Sides are reddish orange. Back scales are spiny. Scales on the thighs are granular. There is usually a dark bar across the shoulder. Male: Light blue mottling on throat and vivid blue patches on belly. **Size:** 5–6⅛ inches (12.7–15.6 cm).

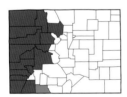

Habitat: Areas with gravelly or sandy soils amid dry shrublands, piñon-juniper woodlands, and mountain forests of ponderosa pine and Douglas-fir.

Distribution: Western Colorado, up to about 7,000 feet; can be found at up to 8,500 feet in the southwest corner of the state.

Field Notes: The sagebrush lizard is well-named for the dry shrubland habitat it prefers. This common lizard often climbs up to perch on junipers and shrubs, sometimes as high as 6 feet. It emerges from hibernation in April and stays active through September. The males are territorial and will defend their turf from other males through bobbing push-ups (to expose the blue on their throats and belly) and occasional chasing and fighting. Males sometimes arch their backs and vibrate rapidly up and down. Ants are this lizard's primary prey.

Legal Status: Nongame species. Up to four individuals can be taken and possessed without a license for noncommercial purposes, though no more than 12 individuals in total of all animals from the list of allowed species can be possessed at any one time.

Desert Spiny Lizard
Sceloporus magister

Field ID: Large, spiny-scaled lizard. Gray-brown, flecked with gold or yellow. Head is yellow or orange. Distinctive black mark on each shoulder. Male: Blue patch on throat and vivid blue or blue-green patches on each side of belly. **Size:** 7–12 inches (17.8–30.5 cm).

Habitat: Arroyos and streams amid shrublands.

Distribution: Far southwestern corner of the state, up to about 5,100 feet.

Field Notes: Spiny lizards often perch in the shrubs and trees that characterize their habitat. They like soft soils beneath desert shrubs and are active during the day from about May through September. Males are very territorial and will challenge other males with bobbing push-ups, chasing, and fighting. The bobbing starts out slowly, with single bobs, then grows more rapid. Males seem to tolerate males of other lizard species, however. Spiny lizards hunt insects, spiders, and other arthropods, and sometimes eat flowers and plant material. They are wary animals that dart quickly into cover if threatened.

Legal Status: Nongame.

Prairie Lizard/Fence Lizard
Sceloporus consobrinus

Field ID: Gray and brown, spiny-scaled lizard. Pale stripes on sides of back and black bars along the stripes. Color and patterns vary widely. Animals with rows of chevrons down the back live in rocky habitats from the northern Front Range to southeastern Colorado. Those with stripes of black flecks inhabit sandy prairies of eastern Colorado. Scales on the back of the thigh are keeled. Male: Vivid blue patches on sides of belly and throat. **Size:** 3½–7½ inches (8.9–19.1 cm).

Habitat: Sunny, rocky habitat from the northern Front Range to southeastern Colorado, and areas of soft, sandy soils amid prairie grasslands in eastern Colorado.

Distribution: Throughout eastern Colorado, up to about 7,000 feet.

Field Notes: The two color patterns of prairie lizard were considered subspecies of the eastern fence lizard until 2002. The form with chevrons usually perches on rocks, trees, and outcrops. The form with stripes is ground-dwelling and prefers areas of open, sandy ground with rocks and shrubs or small plants for cover. If threatened, prairie lizards dart under rocks or into rodent burrows but will soon emerge if they aren't further disturbed. Prairie lizards are active during daylight from April through early November. They may emerge on sunny days during warm periods in winter and early spring. Males challenge others by doing bobbing push-ups to flash the blue patches on their belly and throat. "Bluebelly" is a common nickname.

Legal Status: Nongame species. Up to four individuals can be taken and possessed without a license for noncommercial purposes, though no more than 12 individuals in total of all animals from the list of allowed species can be possessed at any one time.

Plateau Fence Lizard
Sceloporus tristichus

Field ID: Spiny-scaled, light brown to olive or reddish brown lizard. Long tail. Pale stripes with a pattern of darker bars down either side of back. Body pattern is highly variable. Scales on the back of thigh are keeled. Male: Vivid blue patches on sides of belly and throat. **Size:** 3½–7½ inches (8.9–19.1 cm).

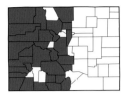

Habitat: Rocky areas of sagebrush and semidesert shrublands, grasslands, piñon-juniper woodlands, canyons.

Distribution: Through western Colorado and the mountains, up to about 7,500 feet; up to 9,200 feet in south-central Colorado.

Field Notes: Along with the prairie lizard, the two main color patterns of plateau fence lizard were once considered subspecies of the eastern fence lizard. There is a lot of variation in color and patterning, some animals being lighter and with fainter patterns and stripes than others, depending on location and habitat. Fence lizards are active during the day from about late March or April through October. They dart and climb well, and may scale the sides of rocks and trees. They hunt by lying in wait or moving slowly toward an insect or other prey, then darting quickly in to grab it. They are fairly tolerant of humans and may sit quietly until approached very closely, then dart off into cover.

Legal Status: Nongame species. Up to four individuals can be taken and possessed without a license for noncommercial purposes, though no more than 12 individuals in total of all animals from the list of allowed species can be possessed at any one time.

The Third Eye

Some spiritual traditions refer to a mystical third eye linked to higher consciousness or used as an amulet to ward off evil. Most Colorado lizards have a third eye, but they use it to regulate body temperature. This parietal eye, located on top of the head, has a lens and retina but cannot register an image. It is very sensitive to changes in dark and light, and acts like a light meter to help the lizard control the amount of time it spends in the sun. A sudden change from light to dark may also mean a predator is about to grab the lizard, so in a way, this third eye probably does help the lizard "ward off evil" by helping it avoid being eaten.

Ornate Tree Lizard
Urosaurus ornatus

Field ID: Small brown to gray lizard. Dark crossbars on back and two bands of abruptly larger scales down middle of back. Tail is long and slender. Defined head and neck. Male: Bright blue, blue-green, or golden patches on sides of belly and a colored throat that can be blue, blue-green, orange, or a mixture. Female: Yellow, greenish, or reddish throat. Fold of skin across throat. **Size:** 4½–6¼ inches (11.4–15.9 cm).

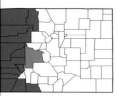

Habitat: Canyons, cliffs, and steep slopes with large boulders; often in piñon-juniper woodlands or shrublands.

Distribution: Throughout most of western Colorado, up to about 8,000 feet.

Field Notes: Tree lizards are agile climbers, able to run up and down the vertical faces of rocks and trees. Despite their name, they are most often found perched on large boulders, though they will climb cottonwoods and other trees in canyon riparian areas. Tree lizards are active from April through October. Males defend their territories against other males, so when two tree lizards are seen together, they are most likely a male and female. During their bobbing display, they bob their entire body up and down on all four legs, unlike the chest raise of many other lizards. This is followed by a series of rapid bobs. The color of the male's belly patches can change depending on temperature.

Legal Status: Nongame species. Up to four individuals can be taken and possessed without a license for noncommercial purposes, though no more than 12 individuals in total of all animals from the list of allowed species can be possessed at any one time.

Common Side-blotched Lizard
Uta stansburiana

Field ID: Small grayish brown lizard. May be unpatterned or have small light and dark spots across its back that lack a significant pattern. Dark blue to black patch on each side of chest, behind the front leg. Fold of skin across throat. Defined neck and head. Male: May have a blue throat with orange around the edge. **Size:** 4–6⅜ inches (10.2–16.2).

Habitat: Rocky canyon slopes and bottoms, arroyos, rocky cliffs and outcroppings, especially amid piñon-juniper woodlands and shrublands.

Distribution: Throughout much of western Colorado, up to about 6,500 feet, and in central-western Colorado to western Eagle County.

Field Notes: The side-blotched lizard is a swift-darting, ground- and rock-dwelling creature. Males don't strongly defend a territory and are much less aggressive than those of other lizard species. They may chase other males and display with bobbing push-ups. They also bob when courting females. These lizards are active during the day from April through October, but in milder areas may become active on sunny winter days. Side-blotched lizards lie in wait for their insect prey, then dart forward to grab them. They consume a great many insects, scorpions, and other invertebrates.

Legal Status: Nongame species. Up to four individuals can be taken and possessed without a license for noncommercial purposes, though no more than 12 individuals in total of all animals from the list of allowed species can be possessed at any one time.

Family Teiidae – Whiptails

The whiptails are ground-dwelling, diurnal, carnivorous lizards with long, thin bodies; sturdy, well-developed legs; narrow heads with pointed snouts; and very long tails that may be one-and-a-half times the length of the body. Most species have distinctive pale stripes running down the body or other patterns of lines and blotches. Their tongues are forked and snakelike. They have eight rows of large, rectangular scales on their undersides and smaller, granular scales on their backs.

Some whiptail species are entirely female, reproducing by parthenogenesis—a type of asexual reproduction in which unfertilized eggs develop into young lizards. These young are the clones, or genetic twins, of the mother. Whiptails are found from the southern United States through South America and on some Caribbean islands. They are very active animals, constantly running, climbing, and even dancing across water to escape danger.

Colorado Checkered Whiptail/
Triploid Checkered Whiptail
Aspidoscelis neotesselata

Field ID: Body and tail of this lizard are long and slim. Back has a pale grayish stripe down the middle and a busy checkered pattern of dark and light spots and bars. Has an unbroken streak on the back of each thigh. Back scales are small and granular; belly scales larger and rectangular. There is a fold of skin with enlarged scales across the throat. Nose is pointed, and there is little differentiation between head and body. **Size:** 4¼ inches (10.8 cm).

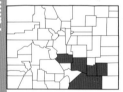

Habitat: Canyons, grasslands, arroyos amid grasslands and shrublands.

Distribution: Southeastern Colorado along the Arkansas River and its southern tributaries, up to about 7,000 feet.

Field Notes: This species consists of all females, which produce eggs that can develop into adults without being fertilized, a process known as parthenogenesis. These whiptails dig burrows for nighttime shelter and use them repeatedly. They lay their eggs in burrows dug in soft soil and will defend these nests afterward. Hatchlings may return to the burrow where they hatched to spend the winter. Formerly known as the triploid checkered whiptail. This lizard is found only in Colorado.

Legal Status: Species of special concern.

Six-lined Racerunner
Aspidoscelis sexlineata

Field ID: This lizard varies from greenish brown to black and may have a bright green wash. Long, slender body and tail. Six to seven pale stripes along back. Back scales are small and granular. No differentiation at the neck between body and head. Male: Green or blue throat and pale blue belly. Female: White throat and whitish belly. **Size:** 6–10½ inches (15.2–26.7 cm).

Habitat: Bare or sparse ground amid prairie grasslands, roadsides, sand-hills, open pine woodlands, and sandy stream banks.

Distribution: Throughout eastern Colorado, up to about 7,500 feet.

Field Notes: This lizard shelters in abandoned rodent burrows and will also dig its own burrows in soft soil. Racerunners are very fast and move all the time. They hunt actively and can be seen darting after insects, especially in the morning. Their movements are jerky, and they often flick their tongues. They have been known to dive into the water to take cover. Competing males flash their blue undersides, vibrate their tails, circle, and bob. They are active during the day from late April through October.

Legal Status: Nongame.

Common Checkered Whiptail/ Diploid Checkered Whiptail
Aspidoscelis tesselata

Field ID: Long, slender lizard with a very long tail and slender, pointed snout. Little differentiation between body and head. Back has small, granular scales. One or two gray to gold stripes running down back; dramatic checkered pattern of dark and light bars between and intersecting the stripes. Legs are dark with many pale spots, including on the back of the thighs. Throat and belly are white. There is a fold of skin with enlarged scales across the throat. **Size:** 11–15½ inches (27.9–39.4 cm).

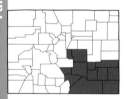

Habitat: Bottoms and slopes of rocky canyons; rock ledges, especially where grassy meadows meet piñon-juniper woodlands.

Distribution: Far southeastern Colorado in Otero, Las Animas, and Baca counties.

Field Notes: All common checkered whiptails are female, and they reproduce by parthenogenesis, meaning eggs develop into adults without being fertilized. This species is active from April through October. Whiptails hunt actively rather than sitting and waiting for prey. They are less wary of humans than other whiptails.

Legal Status: Nongame.

Who's Your Daddy?

Like the mythical Amazon warriors of Greek mythology, three Colorado whiptail lizard species consist entirely of females: the Colorado checkered whiptail, the common checkered whiptail, and the plateau striped whiptail. Young grow from unfertilized eggs into healthy adults. These clones are born "fertile," meaning that since their eggs don't require fertilization, they are born with eggs that are ready to grow into offspring. They have a full complement of chromosomes (eggs that need fertilizing have half the chromosomes) and are complete genetic duplicates of the mother. Because there is no mixing of genes from other animals, these species cannot evolve except through mutation. Biologists don't completely understand this phenomenon, called parthenogenesis, but think it developed in whiptails after two different sexually reproducing species hybridized.

Tiger Whiptail/Western Whiptail
Aspidoscelis tigris

Field ID: Slender, long-tailed lizard with little differentiation between head and body. Body is pale tan or gray with a checkered pattern of dark spots and lines and a series of light stripes. Stripes or spotting are sometimes absent. Back scales are small and granular. Belly and throat are pale, and there is a fold of skin across the throat. Tail is grayish green with black freckles on the sides. **Size:** 8–12 inches (20.3–30.5 cm).

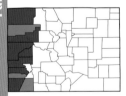

Habitat: Canyons, mesa tops, river valleys, open piñon-juniper woodlands.

Distribution: Western Colorado, up to about 6,000 feet.

Field Notes: The tiger whiptail is mainly a ground-dweller but will climb trees and leap rock to rock. It is active from late April through October. It reproduces sexually, not through parthenogenesis. Courting males will follow females closely. Tiger whiptails dig burrows for cover and to find prey. They keep on the move, actively hunting, and will dart after moving objects, even blowing leaves. Be careful if handling one, as they thrash around and try to bite. This species was formerly known as the western whiptail.

Legal Status: Nongame species. Up to four individuals can be taken and possessed without a license for noncommercial purposes, though no more than 12 individuals in total of all animals from the list of allowed species can be possessed at any one time.

Plateau Striped Whiptail
Aspidoscelis velox

Field ID: Dark, blackish brown lizard with six to seven light stripes along the length of its body. Very long, blue tail (pale in adults, bright in juveniles). Long, slender body and pale or light blue undersides. Back scales are small and granular. There is no indentation at the neck to differentiate between the head and body. **Size:** 8–10¾ inches (20.3–27.3 cm).

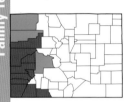

Habitat: Piñon-juniper and ponderosa pine–oak woodlands, shrublands; wooded river and stream corridors.

Distribution: Western Colorado, south of the Roan Plateau, up to about 7,500 feet.

Field Notes: This is an all-female species that reproduces by parthenogenesis, meaning eggs develop into adults without needing to be fertilized. Plateau striped whiptails are active from May through September. They are ground-dwelling lizards and can be approached very closely before they flee; even then they only go a short way. Instead of sitting and waiting for prey to come by, whiptails move around, actively hunting. If captured, they may feign death by going limp. When grabbed, they may whip around and try to bite.

Legal Status: Nongame.

Family Scincidae – Skinks

Skinks are the largest lizard family, with about 1,200 species. Most have long bodies and fairly small legs, though some species have no legs at all. Their necks are not pronounced, giving them a sleek appearance. Most skinks have very long tails that taper to a slender point. The tails will readily break away as a defense against predation, but will regenerate.

Skinks are diurnal but often secretive. They are carnivorous, feeding mainly on insects and other invertebrates. Their pattern of moving can resemble the undulations of snakes rather than the scurrying of lizards. Some of the desert-dwelling species are sand-swimmers, able to burrow into loose sand and "swim" by using muscular undulations of their bodies, similar to the movement of snakes. Many skinks are good burrowers. Others are aquatic or live in trees.

Many-lined Skink/Variable Skink
Plestiodon multivirgatus

Field ID: Small lizard resembling a snake with small legs. Long, slender pale gray to tan body with numerous dark and light stripes. Scales are smooth and shiny with rounded rear edge. Tail is 1½ to 2 times as long as body. Male: Develops orange to red lips in breeding season. **Size:** 5–7¾ inches (12.7–19.7 cm).

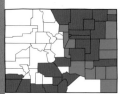

Habitat: Prairie dog towns, open prairie, vacant lots, areas of loose sandy soil, rocky canyons, piñon-juniper woodlands, and oak brush thickets.

Distribution: Northeastern Colorado, north of the Arkansas River, up to about 5,500 feet; in south-central and southwestern Colorado, up to about 8,500 feet.

Field Notes: Considering the length of a skink's body, it's a good thing its tail breaks away easily. The tail of the many-lined skink is as much as two-thirds the animal's total length. The skink is a very shy and secretive lizard and spends much time beneath logs, rocks, and ground litter. It burrows readily and has been found a foot underground. Many-lined skinks are active April through early October. Though common in some areas, not a lot is known about this skink because of its secretive habits. The variable skink is considered a subspecies of the many-lined skink.

Legal Status: Nongame.

Great Plains Skink
Plestiodon obsoletus

Field ID: Large, pale skink with overlapping, dark-edged scales that create a dark-and-light pattern on the back. Scales are smooth and shiny with rounded rear edges. Sides are yellow. Newly hatched young have a coal black body and blue tail.
Size: 6½–13¾ inches (16.5–34.9 cm).

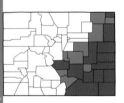

Habitat: Usually near water, along stream, river, and canyon bottoms or irrigation ditches; also on rocky hillsides and rock ledges, sandhills, and around abandoned structures in rural areas.

Distribution: Eastern Colorado, mainly along the Arkansas River drainage, up to about 7,200 feet; also along the Big Sandy Creek in southeastern Colorado, the Republican River in northeastern Colorado, and the South Platte River in extreme northeastern Colorado.

Field Notes: The Great Plains is the largest skink, with a stout body and a tail that is no more than 1½ times the head and body length. It is active May through September. A very secretive lizard, it spends much of its time beneath logs, rocks, and other cover. It emerges into the open only in warm weather and is quite wary. Adults do not have large territories, often inhabiting home ranges no more than about 150 feet in diameter. Be cautious if handling these animals, for they thrash around and bite hard. Many adults show signs of having a regenerated tail.

Legal Status: Nongame.

SNAKES: ORDER SQUAMATA, SUBORDER SERPENTES

Order Squamata, which includes lizards and snakes, is the largest and most diverse order of reptiles, with some 7,000 species. The bodies of these animals are covered with scales, and they all occasionally shed their skin.

Suborder Serpentes encompasses the snakes, which are descended from lizards. Snakes inhabit every continent except Antarctica, as well as most islands. There are about 2,900 species in the world. Snakes have very elongated bodies and no legs, though some species have tiny remnant legs. The tail, an extension of the backbone beyond the body, extends from the vent to the tip. Because of their narrow body design, snakes' inner organs, such as the kidneys, aren't side by side but one in front of the other. Most snakes have only one lung, but they may have up to 400 vertebrae. They have a mobile skull with many joints, and the lower jaw is connected at the front by a flexible ligament. This allows the skull and jaw to expand in order to swallow large prey.

Snakes lack eyelids and external ears or ear openings. Their eyes are protected by a single transparent scale called a spectacle. As an adaptation to their bodies always being in contact with the ground surface, they are extremely sensitive to vibrations.

Note: Measurements for snakes are for total length (TL) from tip of nose to tip of tail.

Family Leptotyphlopidae – Slender Blind Snakes

This family of snakes are small and fossorial, leading to their common names: slender blind, thread, and worm snakes. These shy animals are rarely more than a foot long, and some measure only five inches. Uniformly sized, overlapping smooth scales cover their bodies, and they have tiny vestigial eyes that are just black dots. They have short, blunt snouts and small mouths. The short tail has a sharp spine at the tip. Their few teeth are only on the lower jaw. They live in burrows or crevices and are rarely seen, though they may emerge at dusk to hunt on the surface. They feed mainly on ants and termites.

Slender blind snakes live in tropical areas of North and South America, Africa, and Asia. There are two species in the southern United States; only one inhabits Colorado.

Texas Threadsnake/Texas Blindsnake
Leptotyphlops dulcis

Field ID: Very slender and wormlike. Smooth, shiny reddish brown to pink scales. Eyes are so tiny they look like black dots. There is a short spine at the tip of the tail. **Size:** 5–10¾ inches (12.7–27.3 cm).

Habitat: In damp soil and beneath rocks of canyon sides and canyon bottoms.

Distribution: Southeastern corner of the state, in Baca and Las Animas counties.

Field Notes: Many people might mistake this slender, glistening, seemingly eyeless snake for a giant earthworm. Its short, blunt head, short tail, and smooth, reddish brown to pink scales do give it the look of a large worm. The threadsnake is nocturnal and rarely seen in the open during the day, except after heavy rains that drive it from its hiding place. It is a good burrower. This species was formerly known as the Texas blindsnake because of its tiny, vestigial eyes. It finds its prey by scent, often locating ant colonies by following the ants' scent trail. The threadsnake is also called a worm snake. It is not a common snake in Colorado and has been found in only a few places.

Legal Status: Species of special concern.

Family Colubridae – Nonvenomous Snakes

This widespread family of snakes includes two-thirds to three-fourths of all snake species in the world. Its members are very diverse in appearance, physical characteristics, and lifestyle, and have few traits that are common to all family members. They generally have large heads; large, regular scales; well-developed eyes with vertical pupils; and teeth on both jaws. They live on the ground, in trees, or in and around water. Some of this family, whose members are also referred to as colubrid snakes, produce venom to immobilize prey, but the venom is harmless to humans.

Colubrids inhabit every continent except Antarctica. The root of the family name, *coluber*, comes from the Latin word for snake.

Glossy Snake
Arizona elegans

Field ID: Smooth-scaled, glossy snake with a varied pattern of large black-edged blotches that may be tan, brown, or gray against a pale body color. Belly whitish. Snout fairly pointed. Lower jaw inset. **Size:** 26–56 inches (66–142.2 cm).

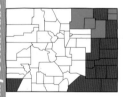

Habitat: Grasslands, sandhills, canyon bottoms, and riparian areas.

Distribution: Eastern Colorado, especially along the Arkansas River, up to 5,000 feet; also in the far southwestern corner of the state.

Field Notes: In some places the glossy snake can reach 70 inches (177.8 cm) total length, but most in Colorado are no more than about 46 inches (116.8 cm)—still a pretty sizable snake. This snake is a good burrower and excavates its own burrow or occupies existing rodent burrows rather than sheltering under rocks or objects on the ground surface. It is active from May through September and is seen above ground in the evening in late spring and summer. Lizards, small rodents, and other animals are its main prey.

Legal Status: Nongame.

North American Racer
Coluber constrictor

Field ID: Large, slender, smooth-scaled snake. Brown, olive, or green with a yellow or cream underside. Juveniles have a pattern of brown blotches. Each nostril is centered across two scales. **Size:** 34–77 inches (86.4–195.6 cm).

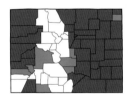

Habitat: Prairie grasslands, sandhills, riparian areas, shrublands, canyons, piñon-juniper woodlands, and agricultural areas adjacent to natural habitat.

Distribution: Throughout eastern Colorado, up to about 6,000 feet; in northwestern Colorado, up to about 5,500 feet.

Field Notes: Racers are well-named, as they are very agile and fast, and are often seen racing across the ground. They spend most of their time on the ground but are good climbers. They are active during the day from early April through September. Females may lay their eggs in communal nests, which sometimes contain dozens of eggs. Racers feed on a variety of prey, including small mammals, birds, lizards, insects, and other snakes. When hunting, they move quickly through the vegetation with their head up. Upon spotting prey, they may dart after it and grab it. Despite their scientific name, racers are not constrictors. They crush prey in their jaws or swallow it alive.

Legal Status: Nongame species. Up to four individuals can be taken and possessed without a license for noncommercial purposes, though no more than 12 individuals in total of all animals from the list of allowed species can be possessed at any one time.

Ring-necked Snake
Diadophis punctatus

Field ID: This smooth gray to olive snake has a yellow belly with black spots. Underside of tail is red or orange. Orange ring or partial ring around neck. **Size:** 10–16½ inches (25.4–41.9 cm).

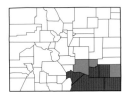

Habitat: Canyon bottoms, riparian areas, prairie grasslands.

Distribution: Southeastern Colorado below 6,000 feet along tributaries of the Arkansas River in Las Animas, Huerfano, Baca, Bent, and Otero counties.

Field Notes: The ring-necked snake is strikingly colored, its bright orange and red underside in dramatic contrast to its drab green or gray back. When threatened, it coils its tail tightly and flashes its colorful underparts, perhaps to warn of the foul-smelling fluid it releases as a defense. Ring-necked snakes are active by day or night from April through September. They are secretive animals, spending much time beneath logs, rocks, and leaf litter. Their diet includes small reptiles, insects, and many earthworms. In the Southwest and Mexico, these snakes can reach 30 inches (76.2 cm) in length.

Legal Status: Nongame.

Great Plains Ratsnake/Corn Snake
Pantherophis emoryi

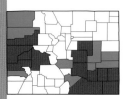

Field ID: Long, slender snake whose background color varies from pale gray to yellowish brown to orange. Middle of back marked with large red, brown, olive, or gray blotches that are edged in black. Smaller blotches on each side. Belly has large, black squares. There are often stripes on the underside of the tail. Wedge-shaped marking on head and a masklike dark chevron across eyes. Scales on back are slightly keeled. **Size:** 24–71 inches (61–180.3 cm).

Habitat: Grasslands and woodlands along canyon bottoms, river and stream courses, arroyos, and ditches.

Distribution: Southeastern and west-central Colorado, up to about 6,000 feet.

Field Notes: This handsome snake is primarily nocturnal but is also seen about in early evening. It is active from May through September. It often enters farm and ranch buildings in search of mice and other rodents. Though ground-dwelling, this snake is also a good climber, scaling trees and finding its way into barn lofts. It can reach 71 inches, nearly 6 feet, in length, but is usually no more than 49 inches long (124.5 cm), and in western Colorado is only up to about 31 inches (78.7 cm). The ratsnake is also called a corn snake, which may refer to its presence around rodent-attracting corn stores, or to the checkered pattern on its belly, reminiscent of kernels of Indian corn. It is rarely far from water.

Legal Status: Nongame.

Shedding Skin

If you crawled around on the ground and over rocks all the time, your clothes would wear out, and that's what happens to the outer skin of a snake. So periodically, a snake must shed that old skin like a worn-out overcoat. Over time, the outer skin toughens and dies, while beneath it the snake is growing a new skin. When the new skin is formed, the old skin begins to dissolve, causing the old outer skin to soften and grow dull. The spectacles—the scales covering the eyes—get cloudy, and until the snake can see again it will strike readily. The snake rubs its head against rocks until the skin comes loose around the lips and from the head. Then it slithers through rocks and vegetation until the skin catches and is pulled off, inside out. Lizards and turtles also shed their skin, but it comes off in patches rather than in one single piece.

Plains Hog-nosed Snake
Heterodon nasicus

Field ID: This stocky-bodied, thick-necked snake has a distinctive upturned, pointed snout. It is gray, brown, tan, or yellowish, with dark blotches (sometimes faded) down the back and spots on the sides. The underside has large black blotches.
Size: 16–20 inches (40.6–50.8 cm).

Habitat: Prairie grasslands and sandhills, often near streams, ditches, and ponds.

Distribution: Throughout eastern Colorado, up to about 6,000 feet; in northwestern Colorado around Maybell in Moffat County.

Field Notes: The hog-nosed snake is distinctive not just for its unusual snout, but also for its dramatic ability to play dead. When threatened, it will hiss and strike (usually with the mouth closed), but if this doesn't drive away the threat, it rolls over with its mouth lolled open and its tongue hanging out. If this "dead" snake is turned upright, it will flip back over to expose its belly and continue feigning death. It may also coil up when frightened, with its head hidden beneath its coils. Though in other areas the hog-nosed snake can reach 36 inches (91.4 cm) in length, most Colorado snakes are no more than 20 inches (50.8 cm) total length. They are active mainly in mornings and evenings, from late April through mid-October. They use their distinctive, spade-shaped snouts to dig after prey.

Legal Status: Nongame species. Up to four individuals can be taken and possessed without a license for noncommercial purposes, though no more than 12 individuals in total of all animals from the list of allowed species can be possessed at any one time.

Chihuahuan Nightsnake
Hypsiglena jani

Field ID: Tan or brown snake with smooth scales and many dark blotches on its back. Very large, prominent blotches on neck; dark bar behind eye. Eyes have vertical pupils. Belly is pale and unmarked. **Size:** 12–24 inches (30.5–61 cm).

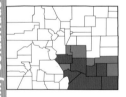

Habitat: Canyons and rocky hillsides with grass, piñon, and juniper.

Distribution: Southeastern Colorado, mainly south of the Arkansas River, up to about 6,000 feet.

Field Notes: The small, secretive nightsnake is well-named, spending the daylight hours hiding under rocks and leaf litter. Lizards are among its main prey. By hunting at night, it takes advantage of a period when the diurnal lizards are inactive and lethargic due to cool temperatures. The nightsnake seizes its prey and holds on, allowing its toxic saliva to slowly immobilize the animal. The saliva isn't dangerous to humans. Nightsnakes are active in Colorado from May through October. They may be common in some areas but are rarely seen because of their shy habits.

Legal Status: Nongame.

Desert Nightsnake
Hypsiglena chlorophaea

Field ID: Small, slender, smooth-scaled snake with a flat, narrow head. Pale gray, beige, brown, or cream, depending upon the soil where it lives, with dark brown blotches on back and sides. There are usually large dark marks on the neck and a dark bar through the eyes. Underside is pale and unmarked. **Size:** 12–26 inches (30.5–66 cm).

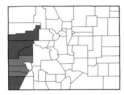

Habitat: Shrublands, grasslands, vacant lots.

Distribution: West-central Colorado, up to 6,600 feet; Mesa Verde National Park.

Field Notes: This nightsnake is true to its name—active at night and at dawn and dusk. It spends much of its time hiding beneath rocks, fallen logs, and other ground debris. The desert nightsnake feeds mainly on lizards and lizard eggs, but also preys on other snakes, frogs, and invertebrates. It is active April through September. Though these snakes can grow to be greater than 2 feet long, most are small, measuring 12 inches (30.5 cm) or less. Few get bigger than 16 inches (40.6 cm). Though this snake is mildly venomous, it doesn't pose a danger to people.

Legal Status: Nongame.

Common Kingsnake
Lampropeltis getula

Field ID: This large, smooth-scaled snake has alternating bands of black and white, or is black with white speckles or blotches. Belly can be white or white with black blotches.
Size: 36–72 inches (91.4–182.9 cm).

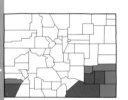

Habitat: Usually near a permanent stream in shrublands; river bottoms; grasslands.

Distribution: Black-and-white banded form found in far southwestern Colorado. Speckled form found in southeastern Colorado, up to about 5,200 feet.

Field Notes: The common kingsnake is a handsome, very dramatically patterned snake. Though widely distributed across the southern United States, there are not a lot of records of kingsnakes in Colorado, perhaps because they live in remote habitat or because the populations are very localized. When found, kingsnakes are often seen on roads. They're also found around farms, ranches, and rural developments. They are active during the day, especially early morning and dusk, from May through September. Kingsnakes are mainly ground-dwellers but can climb into shrubs and trees. King-snakes can reach nearly 84 inches (213.4 cm) in length in some areas, but in Colorado most are no more than about 40 inches (101.6 cm) long. Some taxonomists consider the speckled kingsnake a separate species.

Legal Status: Species of special concern.

Milksnake
Lampropeltis triangulum

Field ID: This smooth-scaled snake is dramatically patterned. Bands of red edged in black alternate with bands of white, cream, or tan down the body. **Size:** 14–34 inches (35.6–86.4 cm).

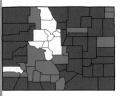

Habitat: Shortgrass prairie, piñon-juniper woodlands, sandhills, open ponderosa pine forest, river valleys.

Distribution: Throughout eastern, southern, and western Colorado, up to about 8,400 feet.

Field Notes: The vividly colored and patterned milksnake is one of Colorado's most handsome snakes. A shy, nocturnal creature, it shelters beneath logs, rocks, and debris during the day, emerging at night to hunt. It is active from April through September. If disturbed, a milksnake will strike, vibrating its tail against dry vegetation to mimic a rattler. Milksnakes can reach 78 inches (198.1 cm), or 6½ feet, in length in some areas, but are generally no more than about 33 inches (83.8 cm) in Colorado. The milksnake's common name derives from the myth that it drinks milk from cows, a story that probably arose because it inhabits farm buildings. It can be mistaken for the venomous coral snake, which has black, yellow, and red bands but does not live in Colorado.

Legal Status: Nongame.

Live Birth? Not Eggzactly

We all know birds lay eggs and mammals give birth to their young. But with reptiles, strategies for having babies are all over the map.

Most reptiles are what is called oviparous (*ovi* = egg; *parous* = birth). They lay shelled eggs, which for most species are leathery rather than hard like bird eggs. But some snakes, such as rattlesnakes, are ovoviviparous (*ovi* = egg; *vivi* = live; *parous* = birth). The female produces eggs but retains the eggs within her body. Though the birth of these babies appears similar to the birth of young mammals, ovoviviparous babies are not connected to the mother's body by a placenta. They mature within a membrane and are nurtured by a yolk sac, as do young maturing within an egg laid outside the mother's body. When they are ready, they hatch from the membrane inside the mother's body and are then born live.

In an additional strategy, snakes such as the smooth greensnake retain the eggs within the mother's body until the young are almost fully developed. The eggs are then laid a few days before hatching.

In some snakes, including the common gartersnake, the young are connected to some degree to the mother's body by a rudimentary placenta. Like mammals, these animals are viviparous (*vivi* = live; *parous* = birth).

With these various strategies, reptiles demonstrate the evolution from laying eggs to the more-advanced nurturing of embryos through a physical connection to the mother, which reaches its greatest development in mammals.

Smooth Greensnake
Opheodrys vernalis

Field ID: This smooth-scaled, uniformly colored snake is bright green with a white underside. Each nostril is centered in a single scale. **Size:** 14–26 inches (35.6–66 cm).

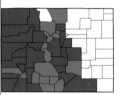

Habitat: Shrubby or grassy montane riparian areas, streamsides, meadows, shrublands.

Distribution: Through central and western Colorado, up to about 9,000 feet.

Field Notes: This colorful snake is a bright grass green. This makes it wonderfully camouflaged in lush grass and thick vegetation but more obvious in arid, drabber environments. Greensnakes often shelter together in groups under rocks and logs. Elsewhere they have been found hibernating in groups of up to 150 snakes. In some areas, they also nest communally. They are active during the day from May through September. Females may retain their fertilized eggs within their bodies, laying them just a few days before hatching. Insects and spiders are the greensnake's main prey.

Legal Status: Nongame.

Coachwhip
Coluber flagellum

Field ID: A very long, lithe, smooth-scaled snake colored brown, pinkish, or red, sometimes with a pattern of dark bars. Scale pattern on tail resembles a braided whip. **Size:** 36–80 inches (91.4–203.2 cm).

Habitat: Shortgrass prairie, shrublands, rocky or grassy hillsides, riparian woodlands, canyon sides.

Distribution: Southeastern Colorado in the Arkansas River drainage; along the Republican River in northeastern Colorado; up to about 6,000 feet.

Field Notes: This species' very long, sinuous body, along with the pattern of cross-braiding on its tail, reminded early westerners of the whip wielded by a coach driver. This not only led to its name, but also led to the myth that this snake whips its prey to death. A very fast snake, the coachwhip is also fairly aggressive and if cornered will strike rapidly and repeatedly, often at the face of its enemy. Though it isn't venomous, the coachwhip can deliver an unpleasant bite. Coachwhips are active during the day from mid-April through mid-October. They forage over large areas, moving very quickly, pausing with the head raised, perhaps to detect danger or possible prey. Though speedy groundsters, they also can climb shrubs and trees. In parts of their range, coachwhips can reach 102 inches (259.1 cm) in length.

Legal Status: Nongame.

Striped Whipsnake
Coluber taeniatus

Field ID: Long, very slender smooth-scaled snake. Gray, brown, or olive, with two or more black and white stripes running the length of each side. White-edged scales create a pattern on the head. **Size:** 40–72 inches (101.6–182.9 cm).

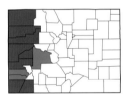

Habitat: Shrublands, mesa tops, piñon-juniper woodlands, canyon bottoms, arroyos.

Distribution: Throughout western Colorado, up to about 8,100 feet.

Field Notes: This extremely fast snake darts around after its prey, often with its head uplifted. If threatened, it disappears in a flash, taking cover in brush, rocks, or animal burrows. Whipsnakes are active during the day from April through early October. Lizards are a major part of their diet. They also hunt snakes, small mammals, and insects. They are not only fast on the ground, they are also agile climbers and will hunt nesting birds. Communal winter dens can contain hundreds of individuals. Whipsnakes usually return to the same den in successive winters.

Legal Status: Nongame.

Northern Watersnake
Nerodia sipedon

Field ID: This sturdy snake is tan or brown with a pattern of pale brown bands that fade into blotches on the rear portion of the body. Underside is white, yellow, or gray, with crescent-shaped black or reddish marks. Old individuals may be very dark, obscuring the pattern. Scales are keeled. **Size:** 22–59 inches (55.9–149.9 cm).

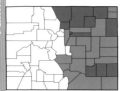

Habitat: Streams, ditches, pools, ponds, wetlands, wet meadows.

Distribution: Along the South Platte, Arkansas, and Republican rivers and tributary streams in eastern Colorado, up to about 5,500 feet.

Field Notes: The watersnake is well-named, as it is often found in water or not far from it. Its body pattern is not dramatic or highly contrasting. Though it can reach 60 inches (152.4 cm) in length, in Colorado it is rarely more than 39 inches (99.1 cm). Because of its banded pattern and the fact that it lives near water, the watersnake is sometimes mistaken for a cottonmouth (which is not found in Colorado), but the watersnake is nonvenomous and shy. If cornered, it will strike repeatedly. An anticoagulant in its saliva will cause bite wounds to bleed profusely. Watersnakes are active day and night from late March through early October. They forage in the water for fish, frogs, toads, tadpoles, and crayfish. Instead of laying eggs, this snake bears live young, which develop within a membrane inside the female's body.

Legal Status: Nongame.

Bullsnake/Gophersnake
Pituophis catenifer

Field ID: This sturdy snake is yellowish or cream colored with a regular, dramatic pattern of dark blotches down the back. The scales are keeled. **Size:** 48–100 inches (121.9–254 cm).

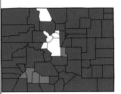

Habitat: Grasslands, shrublands, sandhills, riparian areas, ponds and streamsides, canyons, piñon-juniper woodlands, open ponderosa pine woodlands, farms and ranches.

Distribution: Throughout Colorado, up to about 8,500 feet.

Field Notes: The bullsnake is one of the most-encountered snakes in the state. It lives in a broad range of habitats and is tolerant of habitat changes and human activity. When threatened, the bullsnake coils and raises its head in a defensive posture. It may rattle its tail against dry vegetation, mimicking the sound of a rattlesnake. This has led to the killing of many bullsnakes mistaken for rattlers. Thousands are killed on roads. Others are killed intentionally by people who fear snakes. Because bullsnakes feed on rodents, they are very beneficial and should be protected, especially in agricultural areas. They are active during the day, especially in early morning and at dusk, from April through October.

Legal Status: Nongame species. Up to four individuals can be taken and possessed without a license for noncommercial purposes, though no more than 12 individuals in total of all animals from the list of allowed species can be possessed at any one time.

Look Ma, No Hands

It's amazing to think of climbing trees or swimming without arms or legs. But many snakes can do both of these things well. Snakes move by slithering, using rhythmic contractions of their long, muscular bodies and pushing off against the ground. Their belly scales, which help them grip the surface, can leave a characteristic track in soft soil. Though they can move forward very quickly, snakes cannot slither backward. They swim by undulating across the surface of the water, pushing against the water with each curving movement to propel themselves forward. They climb trees by extending their head and front end, anchoring that around the tree trunk, bringing their tail end up to meet their front, anchoring it, extending the head and front end again, and on and on. Their ancestors had four legs like most vertebrates.

Long-nosed Snake
Rhinocheilus lecontei

Field ID: Reddish or pinkish snake with black saddle-shaped marks down its back and tail. Black and white speckling on sides; white or yellowish underside. Pointed, tapering nose projects over lower jaw and tilts upward at the tip. **Size:** 22–41 inches (55.9–104.1 cm).

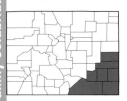

Habitat: Sandhills, prairie grasslands, river valleys.

Distribution: The southeastern corner of the state, up to about 5,000 feet.

Field Notes: This shy and secretive snake is active mainly at night, from mid-May through early September. It is a good burrower and spends the day underground or beneath rocks. When threatened, it may coil and hide its head beneath the coils. If handled, it releases a foul-smelling secretion, like many snakes, but may also bleed from the nose and mouth. Long-nosed snakes feed on lizards, other snakes, rodents, and occasional insects.

Legal Status: Nongame.

Western Groundsnake
Sonora semiannulata

Field ID: A very small, smooth-scaled snake. Pale gray, brown, or orange; saddle-shaped black marks or bands down back. Some groundsnakes have little or no pattern. **Size:** 8–19 inches (20.3–48.3 cm).

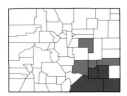

Habitat: Rocky hillsides, rock outcrops, and canyon bottoms amid shortgrass prairie.

Distribution: Southeastern Colorado, up to about 5,500 feet.

Field Notes: This tiny, secretive snake is most often found sheltering beneath rocks and other cover on the ground, often in burrows. It is active from late April through September. It prefers moister conditions and tends to emerge at dusk and into night and sometimes in the morning, as long as temperatures are cool. It retreats into cooler, moister burrows during hot, dry times. Because of its shy habits and small size, the groundsnake is not seen frequently but is probably fairly common. It preys on insects, spiders, centipedes, and other smaller invertebrates. Most groundsnakes are no more than 15 inches (38.1 cm) long.

Legal Status: Nongame.

Smith's Black-headed Snake
Tantilla hobartsmithi

Field ID: Slender, smooth-scaled snake. Uniform light brown; black cap on head. Pinkish or orange stripe down center of belly. Back edge of the cap is straight or rounded. **Size:** 7–15 inches (17.8–38.1 cm).

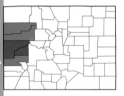

Habitat: Rocky areas of canyon bottoms and slopes, piñon-juniper woodlands, shrublands.

Distribution: West-central Colorado, up to about 6,500 feet.

Field Notes: This small, shy, and secretive snake was once considered rare in Colorado, but its population may actually be quite large. It is active from early May through late August, at dusk and into the night, with the greatest activity just after dark. Like the very similar plains black-headed snake, the Smith's has grooved teeth at the back of the jaw used to hold on to prey as they succumb to the snake's toxic saliva (which is not harmful to humans). It feeds on insect larvae, worms, centipedes, and other small, soft invertebrates.

Legal Status: Nongame.

Plains Black-headed Snake
Tantilla nigriceps

Field ID: Small, smooth-scaled snake. Body is a uniform light brown, with a black cap on the head. Rear edge of cap is pointed. Belly is white. Pinkish or orange stripe down center of underside. **Size:** 7–15 inches (17.8–38.1 cm).

Habitat: Prairie grasslands, sandhills, canyons, foothills.

Distribution: Throughout southeastern Colorado; in northeastern Colorado along tributaries of the South Platte River at the base of the Front Range; in the Republican River drainage; up to about 7,000 feet.

Field Notes: The small and secretive black-headed snake is probably widespread and common in much of eastern Colorado, but goes unnoticed. It is active mainly at night, spending the day in moist hiding places beneath rocks, fallen limbs, tree trunks, or other ground debris, as well as in rotting stumps or logs. It feeds on small, soft-bodied invertebrates, including insect larvae, slugs, and centipedes. There are grooved teeth at the back of its jaw, which it uses to hold on to prey while they are incapacitated by its toxic saliva (which is toxic to invertebrates, but not dangerous to people).

Legal Status: Nongame.

Black-necked Gartersnake
Thamnophis cyrtopsis

Field ID: Greenish brown or greenish gray snake. Yellowish stripe down center of back. Back stripe separates two large, glossy black blotches on neck. Gray head; black bars on upper lip. Pale stripe down each side. Scales are keeled. **Size:** 16–43 inches (40.6–109.2 cm).

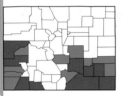

Habitat: Canyon bottoms, streamsides, riparian areas, grasslands near streams.

Distribution: Southeastern Colorado south of the Arkansas River, up to 6,000 feet; southwestern Colorado in western Mesa County and La Plata and Archuleta counties, up to about 6,500 feet.

Field Notes: This handsome gartersnake is active during the day from mid-April through September. It is not common in the state, especially not in western Colorado. It is almost always found along or near water, where it feeds on frogs, toads, tadpoles, small fish, and larval freshwater shrimp. It basks along rocky or brushy streams and swims on the surface of the water rather than below the surface, as do larger, heavier snakes. Like other gartersnakes, it bears live young rather than laying eggs.

Legal Status: Nongame.

Terrestrial Gartersnake
Thamnophis elegans

Field ID: Grayish or greenish snake; pale cream or yellowish stripes down sides of body. Stripe down the center of the back may be bright or faded and may or may not extend the length of the back. Highly variable in appearance and often mistaken for other species of gartersnake. Belly varies from white to blotched and pigmented. Scales are keeled. **Size:** 18–42 inches (45.7–106.7 cm).

Habitat: Grasslands, shrublands, riparian areas, woodlands, wetlands, urban/suburban yards and gardens.

Distribution: Throughout the state, except for the plains of east-central and northeastern Colorado, up to about 11,000 feet.

Field Notes: This familiar gartersnake is found in most of the state and in almost every habitat, including urban and suburban yards, usually along or near water. It often startles home owners and hikers when it slithers suddenly out of grassy yards or vegetation, darting away into cover or across water. It is the highest-altitude reptile in the state, found at up to 11,000 feet, with records of individuals found on the alpine tundra at over 13,000 feet. Gartersnakes eat a variety of prey, including worms, frogs, toads, insects, slugs, and small fish, mice, and birds. They are active during the day from March or April through October or early November. Activity varies with altitude and the onset of the warmer months. Terrestrial gartersnakes bear live young rather than laying eggs.

Legal Status: Nongame species. Up to four individuals can be taken and possessed without a license for noncommercial purposes, though no more than 12 individuals in total of all animals from the list of allowed species can be possessed at any one time.

Western Ribbonsnake
Thamnophis proximus

Field ID: Slender, dark green or grayish snake. Three stripes down body: side stripes are pale, and stripe down middle of back is orange. No black marks on lip scales. Scales are keeled. **Size:** 19–48½ inches (48.3–123.2 cm).

Habitat: Streamsides, ponds, ditches, and other water sources with dense vegetation.

Distribution: Far southeastern Colorado, in Baca County's Furnish Canyon.

Field Notes: The ribbonsnake has been found in Colorado only once, in 1931, in remote Furnish Canyon. It may have been extirpated from the state, or small populations may remain in some remote locations. In other areas, it always lives along water and feeds on frogs, toads, tadpoles, and small fish. Like other gartersnakes, it bears live young. If you are in extreme southeastern Colorado and see this snake, take a photo and report it to the Colorado Division of Wildlife (see *Herpetofaunal Atlas* information on page 159).

Legal Status: Nongame.

Plains Gartersnake
Thamnophis radix

Field ID: Medium-sized, dark green to greenish gray, olive, or black snake with a distinctive central back stripe of orange or yellow and pale side stripes. Row of spots below side stripes. Scales are keeled. Black bars on upper lip. **Size:** 20–40 inches (50.8–101.6 cm).

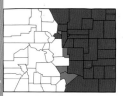

Habitat: Pond, stream, lake, ditch, or reservoir edges; wetlands, marshes, wet meadows, riparian areas, grasslands, sandhills, urban/suburban yards and gardens.

Distribution: Throughout eastern Colorado, up to about 6,000 feet; occasionally found up to 7,500 feet.

Field Notes: This common and familiar snake adapts well to life around humans and human-caused changes to its habitat, and it frequently lives in urban and suburban yards, parks, and gardens. It is active during the day, mainly in the morning, from April through mid-October. Like other garter-snakes, it gives birth to live young instead of laying eggs, and is known to bear as many as 60 offspring. These gartersnakes may gather in large groups at one site where there is a reli-able and abundant food source. When threatened, they dart quickly away into cover or below the water surface. They may

coil and strike, usually without biting. Maximum length in Colorado is usually 36 inches (91.4 cm).

Legal Status: Nongame species. Up to four individuals can be taken and possessed without a license for noncommercial purposes, though no more than 12 individuals in total of all animals from the list of allowed species can be possessed at any one time.

Common Gartersnake/Red-sided Gartersnake
Thamnophis sirtalis

Field ID: This snake is highly varied in its color and can be grayish, greenish, or reddish with darker blotches. Well-defined pale stripe down middle of back; pale side stripes. Scales are keeled. **Size:** 18–51 inches (45.7–129.5 cm).

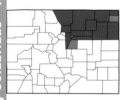

Habitat: Ponds, streams, wetlands, riparian areas.

Distribution: At the base of the Front Range and along the South Platte River, up to about 6,000 feet; along the north fork of the Republican River in Yuma County.

Field Notes: The common gartersnake (though not common in Colorado) is the most broadly distributed snake in North America and is found farther north than any other reptile. It is a water-loving snake, always found in Colorado at the edges of ponds, streams, and waterways, or actually in the water. Frogs, toads, fish, and earthworms are its main prey. Active during the day from mid-March through September, it is one of the first reptiles to emerge from hibernation in spring. It is even known to hibernate submerged in water, allowing the snake to lose less body moisture and conserve energy. They can survive short periods even if the water freezes. If threatened, it readily flees, escaping into vegetation or across or just below the water's surface. It gives birth to live young rather than laying eggs. This snake is also known as the red-sided gartersnake for the reddish color between the stripes.

Legal Status: Species of special concern.

Smelling with Their Tongues

The darting, forked tongue of a snake is frightening to some people, but its purpose is anything but ominous. Snakes have a smell-sensing organ in the roof of their mouth known as a Jacobson's, or vomeronasal, organ. To bring scents to this organ, a snake "sniffs" with its tongue. It darts the tongue out, gathers scent molecules on the tip, and brings the scent to the Jacobson's organ inside its mouth. The organ has two openings, so the forked tongue has two tips. Catch a whiff of that!

Lined Snake
Tropidoclonion lineatum

Field ID: Small, slender snake with keeled scales. Dark gray to light olive with pale sides, a light gray, orange, or yellow back stripe, and a white belly with two rows of black half-moon-shaped marks. Compared to other snakes, the head is small for the body size. **Size:** 12–21 inches (30.5–53.3 cm).

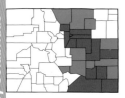

Habitat: Moist areas of grasslands, canyon bottoms, riparian areas; urban/suburban parks, gardens, and yards.

Distribution: Eastern Colorado, especially in the southeastern region of the state, up to about 6,000 feet.

Field Notes: These small, secretive snakes may be more common in the state than records show. They are active in the evening and at night, especially after a rain, from late March through October. Spring and summer rains trigger their activity, bringing them out of daytime hiding places beneath rocks, fallen limbs, leaf debris, and loose soil. If threatened, the lined snake coils, flattens its body, and hides its head beneath its coils. It rarely bites, but releases a foul-smelling fluid from its vent. It feeds mainly on worms. Like the gartersnakes, which it resembles, it bears live young.

Legal Status: Nongame.

Family Viperidae – Vipers

The vipers are venomous snakes found worldwide except in Australia, New Zealand, Ireland, Antarctica, some islands, and from the tropics to above the Arctic Circle. They are carnivorous, using their venom to paralyze and kill prey. They also use it defensively but may conserve venom by delivering a dry bite. All have a pair of hollow or grooved fangs that fold back into the roof of the mouth. When striking, vipers can open their mouths nearly 180 degrees, erecting the hinged fangs. Powerful muscles inject venom into the target.

These sturdy-bodied snakes have short tails and triangular heads that are distinct from the neck. They have keeled scales, slit-shaped pupils, are usually nocturnal, and most give birth to live young. In fact, the term *viper* comes from Latin *vivo* (living) and *pario* (give birth).

Prairie Rattlesnake
Crotalus viridis

Field ID: Large, sturdy, brownish or greenish snake; row of large, dark blotches down middle of back; rows of smaller blotches along sides. Head is very broad; neck is narrow. Scales are keeled. Segmented, horny rattle at end of tail. Highly variable in color and size. **Size:** 16–48 inches (40.6–121.9 cm).

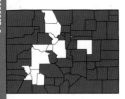

Habitat: Grasslands, shrublands, piñon-juniper and ponderosa pine woodlands, canyons, riparian areas, sandhills.

Distribution: Throughout the state, up to 9,500 feet.

Field Notes: Rattlesnakes figure in story, lore, and the public conscience as probably the most well-known, and feared, snakes in the West. Many are needlessly killed out of this fear, even when not a threat. Prairie rattlesnakes are not aggressive and, when encountered, will escape if possible. Although they may bite without warning if touched or stepped on, when cornered, they will usually coil and rattle their tail, then strike. Rattlesnakes are active mainly during the day, from late April through October, though during the heat of July and August they are more active in the evening and at night. They hibernate in prairie dog burrows, rock crevices, and rodent dens, and may gather in large numbers to overwinter. The rattle is made up of loosely connected, dryish segments. A new "button" is added each time the snake sheds its skin. Contrary to common perception, you can't judge the snake's age by the number of segments. Rattlesnakes give birth to live young.

WARNING: This venomous snake should not be approached or handled.

Legal Status: Game species. Up to three prairie rattlesnakes can be taken daily between June 15 and August 15 with a valid small-game license. A maximum of six rattlesnakes can be possessed at one time. Rattlesnakes can be killed without a license when necessary to protect life or property.

My, You Look Warm Tonight

Snakes see well with their two eyes, but some also "see" heat. Rattlesnakes, which belong to the pit viper family, sense infrared light with heat receptors known as pit organs. They are set in a deep pit on each side of the head, between the nostril and the eye. These pits detect temperature differences between an object and its surroundings. Warm-blooded prey, such as mammals and birds, "shine" against a cooler background, particularly in the evening, when these snakes are out on the prowl.

Midget Faded Rattlesnake/ Western Rattlesnake
Crotalus oreganus concolor

Field ID: Small snake with pattern of large brown blotches down back; smaller blotches on sides. In Colorado, body has a reddish or pinkish tinge. Head is wide and flat; neck is narrow. Horny, segmented rattle on end of tail. **Size:** 16–26 inches (40.6–66 cm).

Habitat: Grasslands, shrublands, canyons, mesas, piñon-juniper woodlands, open coniferous woodlands.

Distribution: West-central Colorado, primarily Mesa, Delta, and Garfield counties.

Field Notes: In Colorado, the western rattlesnake is represented only by a small subspecies, the midget faded rattler, which was formerly considered a subspecies of prairie rattlesnake. It is differentiated from a prairie rattler mainly by its small size, coloration, and limited range. However, identification can be very challenging, as the range of the prairie rattlesnake overlaps that of the midget faded, and prairie rattlers are highly variable in their coloration and size. The habits and behavior of the midget faded rattlesnake are largely the same as those of the prairie rattlesnake.

WARNING: This venomous snake should not be approached or handled.

Legal Status: Species of special concern. Rattlesnakes can be killed without a license when necessary to protect life or property.

Massasauga
Sistrurus catenatus

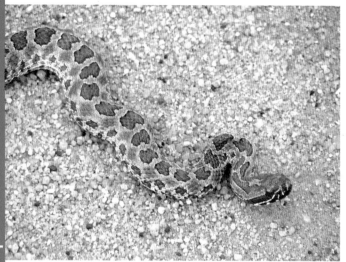

Field ID: Brown or grayish snake; pattern of dark brown blotches down the back, brownish blotches along sides, keeled scales. Nine large, symmetrical scales on the top of the head. Head is broad; neck is narrow. Dark bar with light edges extends from the eye to the back of the jaw. Dark bars on top of the head extend onto the neck. Segmented, horny rattle at end of tail. **Size:** 15–36 inches (38.1–91.4 cm).

Habitat: Grasslands, sandhills.

Distribution: Southeastern Colorado, up to about 5,500 feet.

Field Notes: The word *massasauga* means "great river mouth" in Chippewa, probably referring to the swampy, riverine habitat preferred by eastern populations of massasauga. In Colorado, they are found in dry prairie terrain. Massasaugas are active from mid-April through late October, in the evening and at night in hot weather and during the day when it's cooler. They feed on a variety of prey, including lizards, small rodents, frogs, invertebrates, and bird eggs. These small rattlers are not aggressive but will rattle, coil, and strike defensively if cornered. Their rattle is quieter than that of the prairie or western rattlesnake. Most are no more than 24 inches (61 cm) long. Though massasaugas can reach 36 inches (91.4 cm) in other areas, the average length in Colorado is about 15 inches (38.1 cm).

WARNING: This venomous snake should not be approached or handled.

Legal Status: Species of special concern. Rattlesnakes can be killed without a license when necessary to protect life or property.

Where to See Colorado Reptiles and Amphibians

Populations of reptiles and amphibians have declined dramatically with extensive human development of their habitat. They are small and often secretive and nocturnal creatures, so often they aren't easy to see. Here are some good places in the state to look for them:

- Picketwire Canyonlands – This rocky canyon along the Purgatoire River in southeastern Colorado is a terrific place to see prairie and collared lizards; whiptails; a variety of snakes; softshell and box turtles; spadefoot toads; and various other frogs and toads. Also check out the dinosaur tracks! www.fs.fed.us/r2/psicc/coma

- Carrizo and Cottonwood canyons – Beautiful eastern Colorado canyons that are home to all sorts of lizards, snakes, turtles, frogs, and toads around ponds, streams, and seasonal pools. www.fs.fed.us/r2/psicc/coma, then click "recreation," then "nature viewing," then "viewing wildlife."

- Fountain Creek Regional Park – This park offers Front Range riparian and upland habitat. A good place to look for reptiles including snapping and painted turtles; red-eared sliders; six-lined racerunners; bullsnakes and gartersnakes; as well as leopard and chorus frogs. http://adm.elpasoco.com/Parks/Fountain_Creek_Regional_Trail.htm

- Colorado National Monument – This national park offers great chances to see herptiles, including side-blotched, sagebrush, collared, and plateau fence lizards; bull- and rattlesnakes; and various toads. www.nps.gov/colm

- Rabbit Valley – This desert shrubland habitat above the Colorado River is a good place to see many Great Basin reptiles such as collared, long-nosed leopard, side-blotched, and tree lizards, as well as snakes. www.co.blm.gov

The *Colorado Wildlife Viewing Guide,* by this author, details 201 sites throughout the state to see wildlife.

Become a Citizen Scientist

Here's a chance to get involved with reptiles and amphibians as a citizen scientist. The Colorado Division of Wildlife (CDOW) needs help gathering information on species throughout the state for its *Herpetofaunal Atlas* (http://ndis.nrel.colostate.edu/herpatlas/coherpatlas), a resource they will use for reptile and amphibian conservation. CDOW wants information about all species, from the supercommon to the very rare.

When you encounter an animal in the field, you can record your observation on the atlas, an interactive online database. Compiling data from an army of citizen scientists statewide will add hundreds of records to the knowledge base. Individuals, families, schools, Scout groups, and others are encouraged to get involved.

Here's an overview of the atlas:

- *Online resources* – Species accounts with photos, descriptions, habitat information, recordings of frog and toad songs, and the downloadable *Quick Key to Amphibians and Reptiles in Colorado* are available to help users identify species. There are tips for finding animals in the field as well as a glossary, a Frequently Asked Questions page, and links to other websites and CDOW personnel.
- *Existing database* – Twenty-five thousand historical records offer background information and distribution maps. After your field sightings are validated, they will become a part of this database.
- *Your field observations* – This is the core of the program. You'll need to carefully observe details, so before an outing, download Field Survey sheets. When you return home, log on and submit your field data to the atlas. Each user registers and receives an observer identification number. A major goal of the atlas is to determine where species are distributed in the state, so locations of sightings are essential. Each site will get a location ID so observers can input data for the same sites over successive visits, allowing biologists to track changes year-to-year at a specific site. Take photos, if possible.

To become a citizen scientist with the Colorado Division of Wildlife, visit the atlas website at http://ndis.nrel.colostate.edu/herpatlas/coherpatlas.

Checklist of Colorado Amphibians and Reptiles

Common and scientific names used in this guide are based upon the Society for the Study of Amphibians and Reptiles (SSAR) list of *Scientific and Standard English Names of Amphibians and Reptiles of North America North of Mexico*, Sixth Ed., 2008.

AMPHIBIANS – CLASS AMPHIBIA

Salamanders: Order Caudata
MOLE SALAMANDERS – FAMILY AMBYSTOMATIDAE
- ❐ Barred Tiger Salamander *Ambystoma mavortium*

Frogs and Toads: Order Anura
SPADEFOOT TOADS – FAMILY SCAPHIOPODIDAE
- ❐ Couch's Spadefoot *Scaphiopus couchii*
- ❐ Plains Spadefoot *Spea bombifrons*
- ❐ Great Basin Spadefoot *Spea intermontana*
- ❐ Mexican Spadefoot/New Mexico Spadefoot *Spea multiplicata*

TRUE TOADS – FAMILY BUFONIDAE
- ❐ Boreal Toad/Mountain Toad/Western Toad *Anaxyrus boreas boreas*
- ❐ Great Plains Toad *Anaxyrus cognatus*
- ❐ Green Toad *Anaxyrus debilis*
- ❐ Red-spotted Toad *Anaxyrus punctatus*
- ❐ Woodhouse's Toad *Anaxyrus woodhousii*

NARROW-MOUTHED TOADS – FAMILY MICROHYLIDAE
- ❐ Western Narrow-mouthed Toad *Gastrophryne olivacea*

TREEFROGS – FAMILY HYLIDAE
- ❐ Northern Cricket Frog *Acris crepitans*
- ❐ Canyon Treefrog *Hyla arenicolor*
- ❐ Boreal Chorus Frog *Pseudacris maculata*

TRUE FROGS – FAMILY RANIDAE
- ❐ Plains Leopard Frog *Lithobates blairi*
- ❐ *American Bullfrog *Lithobates catesbeianus*
- ❐ Northern Leopard Frog *Lithobates pipiens*
- ❐ Wood Frog *Lithobates sylvaticus*

REPTILES – CLASS REPTILIA

Turtles: Order Testudines

SNAPPING TURTLES – FAMILY CHELYDRIDAE

- ❏ Snapping Turtle *Chelydra serpentina*

POND AND BOX TURTLES – FAMILY EMYDIDAE

- ❏ Painted Turtle *Chrysemys picta*
- ❏*Red-eared Slider/Pond Slider *Trachemys scripta elegans*
- ❏ Ornate Box Turtle *Terrapene ornata*

MUD AND MUSK TURTLES – FAMILY KINOSTERNIDAE

- ❏ Yellow Mud Turtle *Kinosternon flavescens*

SOFTSHELL TURTLES – FAMILY TRIONYCHIDAE

- ❏ Spiny Softshell *Apalone spinifera*

Lizards: Order Squamata, Suborder Lacertilia

COLLARED AND LEOPARD LIZARDS – FAMILY CROTAPHYTIDAE

- ❏ Eastern Collared Lizard *Crotaphytus collaris*
- ❏ Long-nosed Leopard Lizard *Gambelia wislizenii*

PHRYNOSOMATID LIZARDS – FAMILY PHRYNOSOMATIDAE

- ❏ Common Lesser Earless Lizard *Holbrookia maculata*
- ❏ Texas Horned Lizard *Phrynosoma cornutum*
- ❏ Hernandez's Short-horned Lizard *Phrynosoma hernandesi hernandesi*
- ❏ Round-tailed Horned Lizard *Phrynosoma modestum*
- ❏ Common Sagebrush Lizard *Sceloporus graciosus*
- ❏ Desert Spiny Lizard *Sceloporus magister*
- ❏ Prairie Lizard/Fence Lizard *Sceloporus consobrinus*
- ❏ Plateau Fence Lizard *Sceloporus tristichus*
- ❏ Ornate Tree Lizard *Urosaurus ornatus*
- ❏ Common Side-blotched Lizard *Uta stansburiana*

WHIPTAILS – FAMILY TEIIDAE

- ❏ Colorado Checkered Whiptail/Triploid Checkered Whiptail *Aspidoscelis neotesselata*
- ❏ Six-lined Racerunner *Aspidoscelis sexlineata*
- ❏ Common Checkered Whiptail/Diploid Checkered Whiptail *Aspidoscelis tesselata*
- ❏ Tiger Whiptail/Western Whiptail *Aspidoscelis tigris*
- ❏ Plateau Striped Whiptail *Aspidoscelis velox*

SKINKS – FAMILY SCINCIDAE

- ❏ Many-lined Skink/Variable Skink *Plestiodon multivirgatus*
- ❏ Great Plains Skink *Plestiodon obsoletus*

Snakes: Order Squamata, Suborder Serpentes

*Denotes nonnative species

Look-alikes

Similar Species and How to Tell Them Apart

Many reptile and amphibian species are similar in appearance, and it can be difficult to distinguish one from another. Below is a list of look-alike creatures that present particular identification challenges, and characteristics to tell them apart. Consult each species' description for further details.

Plains Spadefoot Boss directly between the eyes	**Great Basin Spadefoot** Boss between eyes slightly farther back on head

Boreal Toad Lacks cranial crests	**Woodhouse's Toad** Cranial crests

Northern Cricket Frog Restricted range; very rare	**Boreal Chorus Frog** Found statewide

Plains Leopard Frog Skin somewhat rough and warty; folds along sides of back broken and inset at waist	**Northern Leopard Frog** Skin fairly smooth; folds along sides of back not broken or inset at waist

Painted Turtle Smoother, flatter carapace; orange or red plastron with dark marks	**Red-eared Slider** Slightly-keeled, more domed carapace; prominent red "ear" mark; yellow plastron with dark splotches

Common Sagebrush Lizard Sides reddish orange Scales on thighs granular Male has blue mottling on throat, vivid blue patches on belly Limited to western Colorado	**Prairie Lizard** Limited to eastern Colorado	**Plateau Fence Lizard** Scales on thighs keeled. Male has vivid blue patches on throat and sides of belly Limited to western Colorado

Colorado Checkered Whiptail Unbroken pale streak on back of thigh	**Common Checkered Whiptail** Spots on back of thigh	**Tiger Whiptail** Limited to western Colorado

Six-lined Racerunner Limited to eastern Colorado	**Plateau Striped Whiptail** Limited to western Colorado

North American Racer Nostril centered across two scales	**Smooth Greensnake** Nostril centered on a single scale Limited to eastern and far southwestern Colorado

Chihuahuan Nightsnake Limited to southeastern Colorado	**Desert Nightsnake** Limited to western Colorado

Smith's Black-headed Snake Limited to central western Colorado	**Plains Black-headed Snake** Limited to eastern Colorado

Black-necked Gartersnake | Terrestrial Gartersnake | Plains Gartersnake Common Gartersnake | Lined Snake
Closely compare ranges and descriptions

Glossary

Amplexus – The mating embrace of frogs and toads in which the male clasps the female from behind, wrapping his forelegs around her to stimulate her to lay eggs. He then releases sperm over the eggs to fertilize them externally.

Amnion – Fluid-filled sac, similar to an egg but without a hard shell. In some reptiles, young develop within the amnion inside the female's body.

Anuran – A toad or frog

Carapace – The upper part of a turtle's shell; its "back"

CL – Carapace length

Carnivorous – Feeding mainly or exclusively on animal flesh

Cloaca – The internal pouch that collects discharge from the urinary, digestive, and reproductive systems; it opens to the outside through the vent.

Cranial crests – Bony ridges on the head of some toads

Diurnal – Active during the day

Ectothermic – Cold blooded; obtaining body heat from the environment instead of generating it internally

Fang – A long, sharp tooth of snakes, often hollow or grooved to carry venom

Fossorial – Living in the ground; can also mean "adapted for digging"

Gills – Feathery breathing structures found in animals that live in water. These animals, for example the tadpoles and larvae of amphibians, use their gills to extract oxygen from water.

Granular scales – Small scales that feel like grains or pebbles and don't overlap

Herptile – A reptile or amphibian

Hibernaculum – The hibernation den in which animals spend winter or other seasons when few resources are available

Jacobson's organ (also known as the **vomeronasal organ**) – A smell-sensing organ in the roof of a snake's mouth

Keel – A ridge of pointed, bumplike scales found on some snakes and turtles

Larva – The immature stage of amphibians that takes place after the egg hatches but before metamorphosis (for example, tadpoles are larva)

Metamorphosis – The change among amphibians from a gill-bearing, water-dwelling larva to a lung-breathing, terrestrial adult

Musk – Foul-smelling secretions of some turtles, released when the animal is handled

Neotene – An incompletely metamorphosed salamander that can reproduce

Neoteny – The condition in which an incompletely metamorphosed salamander is sexually mature and can reproduce

Nocturnal – Active at night

Oviparous – Laying shelled eggs

Ovoviviparous – Producing soft-shelled eggs that are retained inside the body until the time of birth. The young then hatch from the membrane inside the mother's body and are born live.

Parotoid gland – Poison gland on the neck of some toads, seen as swellings or bumps on the neck behind the eyes

Parthenogenesis – A type of asexual reproduction in which eggs develop into viable young (clones) without being fertilized

Pit organs – Heat receptors in some snakes that are set in a deep pit on each side of the head, between the nostril and the eye

Plastron – The lower part of a turtle's shell; its "belly"

PL – Plastron length

Scutes – The plates covering a turtle's shell

Spectacle – A transparent scale that protects a snake's eyes.

SVL – Snout-to-vent length; the length from the tip of the animal's snout to its vent

TL – Total length; the length from the tip of the animal's snout to the tip of its tail

Tubercle – Small bumps or knobs on the skin of amphibians

Vent – The anal opening through which the urinary, digestive, and reproductive systems all empty

Vestigial – Small and imperfectly developed organ

Viviparous – Bearing live young

Wart – A bump on the skin of toads

Other Resources

Colorado Division of Wildlife *Herpetofaunal Atlas* website
http://ndis.nrel.colostate.edu/herpatlas/coherpatlas

Quick Key to Amphibians and Reptiles of Colorado from the
Colorado Division of Wildlife website (click the link for the
Quick Key)
http://wildlife.state.co.us/Education/ServiceLearning/Herpeto
faunalAtlas/HerpAtlas.htm

The Society for the Study of Amphibians and Reptiles (SSAR)
www.ssarherps.org

The Center for North American Herpetology (CNAH)
www.naherpetology.org

National Biological Information Infrastructure – FrogWeb
www.frogweb.gov

Colorado Natural Heritage Program – Statewide Species and
Natural Community Tracking List
www.cnhp.colostate.edu/download/list/amphibians_reptiles.asp

Colorado Reptile Humane Society
www.corhs.org

About the Author

Award-winning nature writer Mary Taylor Young spent her childhood summers roaming the Colorado Rockies from her grandparents' cabin in Estes Park. Her love of wild things and the outdoors led to a degree in zoology from Colorado State University and a life devoted to nature and the environment. She has written twelve books, including *The Guide to Colorado Birds*, hundreds of magazine and newspaper articles, and works extensively with the US Fish and Wildlife Service, US Forest Service, Colorado Division of Wildlife, and Utah Division of Wildlife Resources. Young lives in Castle Rock, Colorado, with her husband, daughter, two dogs, and many wild neighbors.

About the Photographers

Lauren J. Livo and Steve Wilcox have been taking nature photographs for more than 30 years, specializing in photographs of Colorado's amphibians and reptiles. Their photographs have appeared in books, magazines, posters, and other publications. In addition to her photographic work, Livo has conducted extensive research on western toad ecology as well as geographic distribution and natural history research on numerous other amphibians and reptiles.

Index